ESSEX CCC
On This Day

ESSEX CCC
On This Day

*History, Facts & Figures
from Every Day of the Year*

IAN BROOKES

ESSEX CCC
On This Day
History, Facts & Figures from Every Day of the Year

All statistics, facts and figures are correct as of 31st January 2012

© Ian Brookes

Ian Brookes has asserted his rights in accordance with the Copyright, Designs and Patents Act 1988 to be identified as the author of this work.

Published By:
Pitch Publishing (Brighton) Ltd
A2 Yeoman Gate
Yeoman Way
Durrington
BN13 3QZ

Email: info@pitchpublishing.co.uk
Web: www.pitchpublishing.co.uk

First published 2012

A catalogue record for this book is available from the British Library.

ISBN 978-1-9080514-4-8
Typesetting and origination by Pitch Publishing. Printed in Great Britain. Manufacturing managed by Jellyfish Print Solutions Ltd.

In memory of Frederick Harold Rochester
(1905–1985)
a lifelong follower of Essex cricket

INTRODUCTION

Cricket is a game that combines long periods of waiting with sudden bursts of activity. This is true of a day spent playing or watching the game, but it is also true of the cricketing year as a whole. For the follower of a county club, the opening and closing months of the year involve no competitive action, but may sometimes bring news of the club's preparations for the coming season. Moreover, the performance of the county's players in international cricket in other parts of the world may offer a reminder of the pleasures to be expected in the summer to come. Between April and September, however, there is a complete change of pace, with a daily imperative to keep abreast of the progress of matches. In the summer, it sometimes feels that there is too much going on, but the winter months allow time for reflection and opportunity to put the summer's events into perspective.

In following Essex County Cricket Club through each day of the calendar, this book offers an experience that reflects the cricketing year. The summer months are packed with reports of individual feats and remarkable matches, while the winter months allow time for a longer-term assessment, focusing mainly on the overall careers of players who were born or died on a particular day.

The history of Essex cricket includes many great players and many great characters. The names of Walter Mead, Johnny Douglas, Stan Nichols, Trevor Bailey, Keith Fletcher, Graham Gooch and Alastair Cook naturally feature prominently in this book, reflecting the immense contributions that these players have made to the club. Yet the majority of players who have represented the county in the course of its history have not been international superstars. This book celebrates a few of these men as well. Some made a telling contribution in a brief career; others may not have been successful in top-flight cricket, but their lives are of interest for other reasons. The players who have turned out for the club can boast between them a remarkable array of talents and personas: the artist, the scholar, the soldier, the politician, the businessman, and any number of people who excelled in sports other than cricket. There are stories here of long and fulfilled lives and also stories of lives cut short by war and personal tragedy.

In selecting the material for the book I have tried to include all the great and noteworthy individual performances by Essex players. Perhaps the most surprising theme to emerge from this process is just how many times a supreme individual performance has occurred in a losing cause. Percy Perrin's triple century in 1904 and Mark Ilott's spell of 9 for 19 some 90 years later should both have been enough to win any game of cricket. The same is true of Ryan ten Doeschate hitting a century in a Twenty20 match and Harry Pickett taking all ten Leicestershire wickets for 32 runs. Yet Essex somehow managed to lose not just one of these matches, but all of them. Perhaps the message here is that for all the focus on individual statistics, cricket is very much a team game. Heroic performances linger in the mind, but the overall success of a team depends on contributions from all 11 players.

Of course, the history of Essex also contains some great triumphs. The book records all of the county's championship and one-day titles, the county's highest totals, record partnerships, and biggest wins. I hope that followers of the club will enjoy recollecting these memorable occasions. The history of the club has always been full of interest, and if it has not been one of continuous success, then we should savour the good times all the more.

Ian Brookes

ACKNOWLEDGEMENTS

I am grateful to the many people who fostered (or at least tolerated) my enthusiasm for cricket from an early age, especially to my parents, and to Stewart Mann, who took me to my first county cricket match. John Goodfellow made many excellent suggestions for possible subjects. The task of researching this book has been made easier by the work of earlier historians of Essex cricket, especially Charles Bray, David Lemmon, and Mike Marshall, while I have also made extensive use of the excellent Cricket Archive and Cricinfo websites.

Most of all, I am grateful to Jane Goodfellow for unfailing moral and technical support and for saving me from numerous errors.

ESSEX CCC
On This Day

JANUARY

SUNDAY 1st JANUARY 1905

George Hockey was born in Ipswich. He played in 19 matches for Essex as an amateur between 1928 and 1931 but managed a top score of just 23 and never took a wicket. He later played Minor Counties cricket for his native Suffolk. He died in Bulawayo, Zimbabwe, in 1990 at the age of 85.

WEDNESDAY 2nd JANUARY 1974

Matt Walker was born in Gravesend. He joined Essex in 2009 after playing 15 seasons for Kent, and scored over 1,000 runs in his first County Championship season, including two centuries, as the county gained promotion from the second division. Perhaps his most memorable innings for Essex was the unbeaten 74 from just 49 balls that helped see the county home in the quarter-final of the Friends Provident Twenty20 against Lancashire in 2010.

SUNDAY 3rd JANUARY 1999

Former Essex batsman Stanley Proffitt died in Middleton, Lancashire, at the age of 88. A native Lancastrian, he played a single season for Essex in 1937, when he scored 170 runs in 14 innings at an average of 12.14. He was better known as an international table tennis player, and in his will he left money to fund the Stanley Proffitt Award, given internationally to help the development of young players in the sport.

SATURDAY 4th JANUARY 1913

Jack Dennis was born in Leytonstone. A middle-order batsman, he made his debut against Glamorgan in 1934, but had to wait a further two seasons before playing his second game. He featured more prominently as a member of the first XI in 1937 and 1938, and even captained the side on two occasions in the absence of Tom Pearce and Denys Wilcox. His only half-century came when he made 53 in the first innings of a drawn game against Sussex in 1937, putting on 153 for the sixth wicket with Pearce. In all he scored 530 runs in 33 innings for the county at an average of 17.66 before his first-class career was cut short by the outbreak of war at the end of the 1939 season.

TUESDAY 5th JANUARY 1892

Arthur Bradfield was born in Box, Wiltshire. He kept wicket for Essex four times in the 1922 season, taking two catches and three stumpings. This was not an era when a side relied on its wicketkeeper to contribute with the bat and Bradfield was a confirmed number 11, managing just seven runs in four completed innings.

WEDNESDAY 5th JANUARY 2011

Alastair Cook completed his third century of the Ashes series to set up a crushing victory for England in the final Test at Sydney. Resuming on 61 not out, he took his score to a mammoth 189, including 16 fours. His sixth-wicket partnership of 154 with Ian Bell took the game away from Australia, and England eventually won by an innings and 83 runs. Cook's innings earned him the man of the match award, and took his tally for the series to a mind-boggling 766 runs at an average of 127.66. This was the second-highest aggregate ever by an Englishman in a Test series, earning him the Compton-Miller medal as the player of the series.

SUNDAY 6th JANUARY 1980

Graham Napier was born in Colchester. A hard-hitting batsman and economical seam bowler, his career has been interrupted by injuries. Nevertheless, by the end of the 2011 season he had scored 3,733 runs in first-class cricket at an average of 30.34 and taken 238 wickets. He will be forever remembered by Essex supporters for two outstanding feats of hitting: the astonishing 152 against Sussex in a Twenty20 Cup match in 2008, which featured 16 sixes, and his career-best 196 against Surrey in the County Championship in 2011, when again he cleared the ropes on 16 occasions, equalling the record for a first-class innings.

FRIDAY 7th JANUARY 1876

The *Chelmsford Chronicle* carried an announcement of a public meeting to be held in the Shire Hall on the following Friday "to consider the desirability of forming a county cricket club, with a ground at Brentwood". One of the signatories of the announcement was James Round, who was to become the driving force in establishing the club.

THURSDAY 7th JANUARY 1965

Former Essex captain Paul Prichard was born in Brentwood. He made his debut in 1984 and played 18 seasons for the county, scoring 16,786 runs at 34.46, passing 1,000 in a season eight times, and hitting 32 centuries. In 1995 he took over the captaincy from Graham Gooch and led the side for four seasons, lifting the NatWest Trophy in 1997 and the Benson and Hedges Cup in the following year. He featured in the highest partnership in Essex's history, adding 403 with Gooch against Leicestershire in 1990, recording a career-best score of 245. However, he will perhaps best be remembered for the catch he took to clinch victory in the 1985 NatWest Trophy final.

THURSDAY 8th JANUARY 1925

Johnny Douglas played his last Test innings as England slid to defeat against Australia in the second Test at Melbourne. Set 372 to win, England resumed on 259 for 6. Hopes of an England victory seemed to rest on Douglas being able to support Herbert Sutcliffe, who was unbeaten on 117 overnight. However, the pair added just 21 more runs before Sutcliffe fell, and Douglas soon followed for a disappointing 14 as Australia won by 81 runs.

MONDAY 9th JANUARY 1871

Charles Kortright was born at Furze Hall, near Ingatestone. He played 160 first-class matches for the county between 1894 and 1907, taking 440 wickets at an average of 20.53. He had the distinction of bowling the first ball by an Essex player in the County Championship against Warwickshire in 1895, and took 8 for 94 as Essex forced their opponents to follow on. He was noted as the fastest bowler of his time, and there is a story that he once bowled a bouncer that went over the head of batsman and wicketkeeper and was still rising as it crashed into the sightscreen. That story should probably not be taken too seriously, but nevertheless John Arlott included him among his team of the 11 best players never to have played for England. He was also a useful batsman, who scored 4,182 first-class runs, including two centuries. He succeeded Hugh Owen as captain of Essex, and led the side through the 1903 season.

SATURDAY 9th JANUARY 1875

Edward Russell, the younger brother of Tom Russell, was born in Leytonstone. He played 130 matches between 1898 and 1910, initially as a batsman, but gradually took over the wicketkeeping duties from his brother, who retired in 1905. His career batting average was just over 13 but he did make one century, against Derbyshire in 1901.

MONDAY 10th JANUARY 1887

One of the lesser-known players to have represented the county, Oswald Martyn, was born in Clapham. He made his only appearance aged 35 against Northamptonshire at Southend in 1922. Batting at four, he was caught at the wicket without scoring as Essex collapsed from 50 for 1 to 50 for 6. Happily, however, Essex recovered to take a first-innings lead, and Martyn had the satisfaction of taking a catch in Northamptonshire's second innings. Less happily, he never got the chance to bat again, as Essex secured victory by ten wickets.

SATURDAY 11th JANUARY 1947

Edward Connor died in Enfield, at the age of 74. He made little mark as a medium-pace bowler in two County Championship matches for Essex at the end of the 1905 season, taking just two wickets at an average of 65.50. He served on the ground-staff at Leyton for many years and was awarded a benefit by the county in 1933.

TUESDAY 12th JANUARY 1904

Brian Warsop was born in Willesden, Middlesex. A right-hand batsman and slow left-arm bowler, he played five matches for Essex in 1931 and 1932. Curiously, all of the games were away fixtures against Midland counties, and he never played on a winning side. In all, he made 128 runs at an average of 16, with a top score of 51 against Warwickshire, and bowled six overs without taking a wicket. However, his chief occupation was in the family firm of Warsop and Sons (later to become Warsop Stebbing), a noted manufacturer of cricket bats. In 1933 he left England for Australia to set up a venture importing part-made bats and finishing them. He died in Melbourne in 1993 at the age of 89.

SUNDAY 13th JANUARY 1985

Essex bowler Neil Foster took six wickets as England bowled India out for 272 on the first day of the fourth Test in Madras (now Chennai). Foster's contribution proved to be a critical factor as England went on to win the match and the series. Double centuries from Graeme Fowler and Mike Gatting helped them pile up a huge score, and when India batted a second time Foster was again outstanding, removing Gavaskar, Vengsarkar, and Srikkanth with the new ball. He finished with match figures of 11 for 163 as England won by nine wickets — not a bad effort for a player who had only come into the side as a result of injuries to Paul Allott and Richard Ellison.

FRIDAY 14th JANUARY 1876

A momentous day for the county, as Essex County Cricket Club was formed at a public meeting in the Shire Hall, Chelmsford. James Round, the Member of Parliament for East Essex, took the chair and was to emerge as the club's first chairman, treasurer, and first-team captain, while JF Lescher was appointed honorary secretary. It was decided to set an annual subscription for members of one guinea. By the start of the season £700 had been raised in subscriptions, and the club had entered into an agreement to rent a ground at Brentwood.

SATURDAY 14th JANUARY 1950

Brian Hardie was born in Stenhousemuir, Scotland. He followed in the footsteps of his father and brother in playing cricket for Scotland before joining Essex in 1973. In a career that lasted until 1990, he made over 18,000 first-class runs at an average of 34.22 with 27 centuries, passing 1,000 runs in a season 11 times. His batting was not always in accordance with the textbook, and his unorthodox style often proved a source of frustration to opposing bowlers, not least to the great West Indian Malcolm Marshall, who saw the Scotsman as a personal nemesis: "Whenever Essex play I bowl quick in order to get Hardie. If Hardie open, I bowl fast with the new ball. If Hardie bat in the middle order, I bowl extra fast to get rid of early order, to get to Hardie."

MONDAY 15th JANUARY 1996

Lindsay "Jerry" Jerman died at Chelmsford at the age of 80. He opened the bowling for Essex against the Combined Services in 1950 and in two championship matches in the following season without conspicuous success, but in later years contributed greatly to the funding of the club as chairman of the Essex Development Association.

FRIDAY 16th JANUARY 1953

Keith Pont was born in Wanstead. A stalwart of the successful sides of the 1970s and 1980s, he played 198 first-class matches for Essex, scoring 6,558 runs at an average of 25.12 and taking 96 wickets with his medium-paced bowling at an average of 33.21. He made seven centuries and twice took five wickets in an innings. He excelled especially in limited-overs cricket as a powerful striker of the ball and a fine fielder. His younger brother Ian also played for the county, while his older brother, Kevin Pont, had played for the second XI.

MONDAY 17th JANUARY 1921

Essex batsman Jack Russell scored his first Test century — 135 not out to help England to a first-innings lead against Australia in the third Test at Adelaide. The innings contained a six and 12 fours, and featured a stand of 124 for the sixth wicket with Johnny Douglas, who scored 60. However, Australia were to run up a small matter of 582 in their second innings, with centuries from Kelleway, Armstrong, and Pellew, and despite a century from Jack Hobbs and further contributions from Russell (59) and Douglas (32), England fell 119 runs short of their target. The 1921 series was to be a chastening one for England, who lost 5-0 under Douglas's captaincy, but Russell emerged with an enhanced reputation. He would score a further four Test hundreds, averaging 56.87 in his ten matches.

THURSDAY 18th JANUARY 1917

Harry Pickering was born in Hackney. An opening batsman by trade, he played three matches for the county in 1938, but averaged just 10.33, with a highest score of 17. After the war he played five matches for Leicestershire, recording three half-centuries.

WEDNESDAY 19th JANUARY 1910

Cecil Boswell was born in Edmonton. He played 30 matches for Essex between 1932 and 1936 and took 36 wickets with his leg breaks and googlies at an average of 37.36. His best bowling was a haul of 4 for 22 against Northamptonshire at Colchester in 1935, a performance that helped set up an improbable win for Essex after they had been bowled out for 60 in their first innings. He also managed a single half-century, scoring 69 against Gloucestershire in 1934, when he supported Stan Nichols in an eighth-wicket stand of 134. He later played Minor Counties cricket for Norfolk, where he died in 1985.

FRIDAY 20th JANUARY 1899

Leslie Phillips — no, not that Leslie Phillips — was born in Leyton. He played three championship games over three seasons for Essex, but never scored more than 19 and failed to take a wicket with his slow left-arm bowling. Perhaps they should have tried the other Leslie Phillips.

SUNDAY 20th JANUARY 1971

Keith Butler was born in Camden Town. He is one of the rare players never to have been dismissed in first-class cricket, scoring 10 not out for Essex against Cambridge University in his only match in 1989. He had been awarded his second XI cap the previous summer as a 17-year-old, and went on to play for England Young Cricketers, rubbing shoulders with the likes of Darren Gough, Ronnie Irani and Dominic Cork. Hampered by injury, he played a handful of one-day matches for Essex, but never appeared in the County Championship. In 1993 he joined Suffolk, who were coincidentally drawn against Essex in that year's NatWest Trophy. Butler scored 17 as Essex won easily.

THURSDAY 21st JANUARY 2010

The *Eastern Daily Press* announced that Essex bowling coach Graeme Welch had decided to leave the club. He joined the staff in 2007 after a playing career with Warwickshire and Derbyshire, and cited a desire to be closer to his family in the midlands as the cause of his departure. He became bowling coach at Warwickshire and was replaced at Essex by Chris Silverwood.

CHRIS SILVERWOOD JOINED ESSEX CCC AS BOWLING COACH IN JANUARY 2010

SUNDAY 22nd JANUARY 1893

Patrick Barrow was born in Plaistow. He played Minor Counties cricket for Dorset either side of the First World War, and featured for Essex in a single game against the Combined Services at Leyton in 1922, taking one wicket for 43 runs, but failing to score in his only innings. Aside from cricket, he was a talented composer and an international ice-hockey player.

SUNDAY 23rd JANUARY 1881

Colin McIver was born in Hong Kong. He played a handful of matches for Essex as a batsman in 1902 and 1904, while a student at Oxford University, then re-emerged in 1913 as the side's regular wicketkeeper and opening batsman. He and Jack Russell put on 210 for the first wicket against Hampshire at Leyton, with McIver making a career-best 134. His second Essex career was interrupted by the war, but he continued to play until 1922. In all, he played in 59 first-class matches for Essex, scoring 2,544 runs and taking 43 catches and 13 stumpings.

SATURDAY 24th JANUARY 1880

Arnold Read was born in Snaresbrook into a cricketing family. His father, also called Arnold, played for the county club in the 1880s. The younger Arnold Read played in 22 matches for Essex between 1904 and 1910, with a top score of 70 against Warwickshire in 1905. He was principally a bowler, and in 1908 produced a match-winning performance when he took 7 for 75 on the last day to seal an innings victory over Northamptonshire. His achievements were eclipsed by those of his son, Hopper Read, who became one of the county's most celebrated players.

WEDNESDAY 25th JANUARY 1956

Mike McEvoy was born in Jorhat in the Indian state of Assam. He made his debut in 1976 and played 43 matches for Essex, scoring 1,371 runs at an average of 18.78 with a top score of 67 not out. He left the club after the 1981 season, and later played for Cambridgeshire, Worcestershire, and Suffolk. In 2007, he was a surprising inclusion in a fantasy Essex XI selected by sportswriter Patrick Kidd for *The Times*.

WEDNESDAY 26th JANUARY 1983

Scott Brant was born in Harare, Zimbabwe. He moved to Australia as a teenager and made his debut for Queensland in 2002. He joined Essex as an overseas player in 2003, and in his first season took 37 wickets at 30.18 with his left-arm fast-medium bowling. Returning the following summer, he was troubled by injuries and took only 12 wickets at 55.50. He left at the end of 2004, reluctant to commit to playing a further full season in England.

MONDAY 27th JANUARY 1879

Dan Reese was born in Christchurch, New Zealand. A left-handed all-rounder, he played eight matches for the county in 1906, taking six wickets at an average of 27.50 and scoring 198 runs at an average of 15.23. He then returned to New Zealand, where he represented his country 12 times — eight as captain — in the period before the country's games were recognised as Test matches. He later served as president of the Canterbury Cricket Association.

THURSDAY 27th JANUARY 1966

Steve Andrew was born in Marylebone. He first played county cricket for Hampshire, but moved to Essex in 1990 and played 75 first-class matches for the club over eight seasons. His finest performance came in a rain-affected match against Lancashire at Old Trafford in 1993, when he outshone team-mates Neil Foster, Derek Pringle, and Mark Illot in taking 7 for 47.

FRIDAY 28th JANUARY 1910

Holcombe "Hopper" Read was born in Woodford Green. After playing a single match in 1933, he made a dramatic impression the following year when he was drafted into the side to play Surrey as Ken Farnes and Stan Nichols were both involved in the Test trial. He soon demonstrated his pace by knocking Jack Hobbs' cap off with his first ball and clean bowling him with the last ball of his first over. He played only 32 matches for the county before quitting to pursue a career as an accountant, but in that spell he took 131 wickets at an average of 21.10, and was regarded as the quickest bowler in the world.

TUESDAY 28th JANUARY 1947

Tony Jorden was born in Radlett, Hertfordshire. He came into the Essex side as a teenager in 1966, and played 60 matches between then and 1970, helping to supplement a seam attack that was depleted by the retirement of Trevor Bailey and the departure of Barry Knight to Leicestershire. His appearances from 1968 to 1970 were limited by his commitments at Cambridge University, where he became captain of the side. Meanwhile, the emergence of Keith Boyce, John Lever, and Stuart Turner made him surplus to requirements at Essex. He was also an outstanding rugby player and won seven caps for England at full-back.

SATURDAY 29th JANUARY 1994

George Carter died in Siesta Key, Florida, aged 92. He played six matches for Essex in the 1921 season, and another in 1923 against the touring West Indians. In these, he scored 163 runs at an average of 16.30, the highest score being an unbeaten 44 against Northamptonshire at Leyton.

WEDNESDAY 30th JANUARY 1974

Robert Rollins was born in Plaistow. He made his Essex debut in 1992, and established himself as the side's regular wicketkeeper in the mid-1990s. He played 69 first-class matches, scoring 2,258 runs at an average of 22.35, with 158 catches and 21 stumpings. His only century came against Glamorgan in 1995, when he finished unbeaten on 133.

TUESDAY 31st JANUARY 1995

Essex stars of the past and future found themselves in the middle of a controversy while captaining their respective countries in the first Test between Zimbabwe and Pakistan at Harare. Saleem Malik called "bird" rather than the customary heads or tails as Andy Flower tossed the coin at the start of the game. When the coin fell as tails — the side of the coin adorned by an eagle — Malik assumed that he had won, but match referee Jackie Hendriks ordered the toss to be repeated. This time the Pakistani skipper lost, and by the end of the day Flower had completed a century to set his side on the way to an innings victory.

ESSEX CCC
On This Day

FEBRUARY

SUNDAY 1st FEBRUARY 1948

Walter Turner died in Harrow at the age of 66. He had been born into a military family in India, and followed his more illustrious brother Johnny Turner into the Essex side. His first-class career spanned 27 years from 1899 to 1926, but his appearances were limited by his duties in the army. He played just 48 games for the county, scoring 2,004 runs at 27.08 and hitting two centuries. His highest score came against Middlesex at Leyton in 1919, when he went in with the score at 14 for 3 and rescued the innings with a score of 172 in 165 minutes.

WEDNESDAY 1st FEBRUARY 1995

Future Essex player Grant Flower made his highest Test score of 201 not out against Pakistan in Harare. His innings had begun on the previous day and occupied a mammoth 523 balls. He shared in partnerships of 269 with his brother, Andy, and 233 with Guy Whittall as Zimbabwe declared on 544 for 4.

MONDAY 2nd FEBRUARY 2004

England pace bowler Darren Gough signed for Essex after a much publicised falling out with his native county Yorkshire. Five other counties had expressed an interest in signing the 33-year-old, but his close friendship with Paul Grayson and respect for his former England captain Nasser Hussain made Essex an obvious choice. He would play 24 first-class matches for the county over the next three years, taking 82 wickets at 27.26. At this stage of his career, however, his main strength was in limited-overs matches. In 2007, having made peace with Yorkshire, he returned to Headingley to finish his career.

TUESDAY 3rd FEBRUARY 1998

Mark Waugh saved the third Test for Australia with a battling innings against South Africa at the Adelaide Oval. Fighting to hold on to a 1-0 series lead, Australia were set a victory target of 361 and began the last day in trouble on 32 for 2. Waugh resumed on 11 not out and batted throughout the day, finishing with an unbeaten 115 from 404 balls as Australia held on for the draw with seven wickets down.

FRIDAY 4th FEBRUARY 1955

Percy Toone died in Isleworth, Middlesex, at the age of 71. He played 29 matches for Essex between 1912 and 1922 and took 62 wickets at 31.51 including a hat-trick against Kent in 1920. In the winter months he played professional football, keeping goal for several teams, including Woolwich Arsenal and Southend United.

SATURDAY 5th FEBRUARY 1876

Harding "Sailor" Young was born in Leyton. A left-arm bowler, he played 128 matches between 1898 and 1912, taking 368 wickets at an average of 24.70 and three times took ten in a match. He acquired his nickname when Essex chairman Charles Green bought him out of the navy so that he could play for the county. In 1899 he became the second Essex player, after Walter Mead, to win an England cap, and took 12 wickets in the two Tests he played against Australia. He later became a Test umpire.

SATURDAY 5th FEBRUARY 1944

Graham Saville was born in Leytonstone. He preceded his cousin Graham Gooch in the Essex side by a decade, playing 124 matches in two spells between 1963 and 1966 and then from 1970 to 1974. In the interim he played Minor Counties cricket for Norfolk. He scored 4,265 runs for Essex at 23.05, including two centuries, and after his retirement he continued to serve the club as assistant cricket secretary.

FRIDAY 6th FEBRUARY 1953

Former Essex captain Denys Wilcox died at Westcliff-on-Sea aged 42. He first played for Essex in 1928 as a schoolboy and later played for Cambridge University for three seasons, captaining the side in his final year. After leaving Cambridge he became headmaster of Alleyn Court Preparatory School in Westcliff — the interview presumably made easier by the fact that his father had founded the school. His teaching duties restricted the number of games he could play for Essex, but he nevertheless accepted a share of the captaincy in 1933, and led the side for the second part of each summer until 1939. He played a total of 118 matches for the county, scoring 5,482 runs at 30.79, including eight centuries.

MONDAY 6th FEBRUARY 1995

Graham Gooch played his last Test innings, caught and bowled for four by Terry Alderman in the fifth Test at Perth. England finished the day on a miserable 27 for 5, lurching towards a 329-run defeat. Gooch's four runs took his final Test aggregate to 8,900, which remains the most by any England player.

MONDAY 7th FEBRUARY 1972

Aftab Habib was born in Reading. He established himself as a prolific middle-order batsman with Leicestershire and was selected by England for two Test matches against New Zealand in 1999, but scored only 26 runs in three innings. In 2002 he moved to Essex in a bid to regain his England place, and he played for the county for three seasons before rejoining Leicestershire. In 42 first-class matches for Essex he scored 2,478 runs at 38.12, including five centuries, but he never came close to international selection again.

SUNDAY 8th FEBRUARY 2005

Essex announced the signing of Alex Tudor on a one-year contract. The bowler had been released by Surrey the previous year after an injury-plagued career in which he had shown immense promise and played in ten Tests for England, famously scoring 99 not out as a night-watchman against New Zealand in 1999. He was still only 27 when he signed for the county, but continued to struggle for fitness, managing just three first-class games in his first season. He played a further 27 matches over the next three years before returning to Surrey, taking five wickets in an innings only once, but scoring a century against Derbyshire in 2006.

THURSDAY 9th FEBRUARY 1922

Jim Laker was born in Frizinghall, Yorkshire. He joined Essex in 1962 at the age of 40 after a glittering career with Surrey and England in which he took 193 Test wickets at 21.24. He played in 30 matches for the county over three seasons, taking 111 wickets at 21.32. He took five wickets in an innings seven times, with a best performance of 7 for 73 (and 13 for 159 in the match) against Kent at Dover in 1962.

THURSDAY 9th FEBRUARY 1933

Charles Williams was born in Oxford. He first played for Essex in 1954 while he was a student at Oxford University, and he captained Oxford the following year. He played a total of 40 matches for the county, scoring 1,518 runs at 23.35. His only century came at Leicester in 1955, when he put on 200 for the fourth wicket with Doug Insole. He later had a highly successful business career and in 1985 he became a member of the House of Lords as Baron Williams of Elvel. Lord Williams has also written a number of biographies, including a life of Don Bradman.

WEDNESDAY 9th FEBRUARY 1938

Paddy Phelan was born in Chingford. He played 154 matches for Essex between 1958 and 1965, taking 300 wickets with his off-breaks at 28.86. He also made three half-centuries. He produced several match-winning performances, taking 5 for 22 in his debut season as Northamptonshire, needing 190 to win, were all out for 118, and then in his final season taking 7 for 80 to bowl out Worcestershire. After leaving Essex he played club cricket and raced classic motorcycles.

THURSDAY 10th FEBRUARY 1972

Michael Kasprowicz was born in Brisbane, Australia. He was still uncapped when he replaced Saleem Malik as Essex's overseas player in 1994, but would go on to play 38 Tests for Australia. He played a single season for the county, taking 60 first-class wickets in 17 matches at 31.15. He is probably best known to English cricket followers as being the last man out in England's nail-biting two-run victory over Australia at the Edgbaston Test in 2005.

THURSDAY 10th FEBRUARY 2011

Essex legend Trevor Bailey died in a fire at his home in Westcliff-on-Sea, aged 87. Firefighters were able to rescue his wife, but found Bailey's body in the kitchen of his flat, where it is believed that an electrical appliance had caught fire. His death brought tributes from all around the cricketing world from people who remembered him affectionately as both a great player and a radio commentator on the sport.

MONDAY 11th FEBRUARY 1957

Augustus "Joe" Hipkin died in Carluke, Lanarkshire, aged 56. A slow left-arm bowler, he was born in Norfolk and first played for Essex in 1923. He played 231 matches over nine seasons for the club, taking 518 wickets at 25.82, including a hat-trick against Lancashire in 1924. He also scored 4,239 runs at 15.64, and in 1927 hit centuries against both Glamorgan and Oxford University. He was a talented all-round sportsman, also playing professional football, but many believed he lacked the temperament to make the very best of his considerable ability.

SUNDAY 12th FEBRUARY 1871

Charlie McGahey was born in Hackney. One of the great characters of Essex cricket, he played 400 matches for the county between 1894 and 1921, playing his last game when he was 50. In these he scored 19,079 runs at 30.57, with 29 centuries and a top score of 277 against Derbyshire in 1905. He also developed into a useful leg-break bowler, taking 306 wickets at 30.98 with a best of 7 for 27 against Nottinghamshire in 1906. He was named as one of *Wisden's* Cricketers of the Year in 1902, the year in which he played two Test matches on England's tour of Australia. He succeeded Frederick Fane as captain of Essex in 1907 and led the side for four seasons. After he retired from playing he served the county as assistant secretary and scorer.

SUNDAY 13th FEBRUARY 1898

Hubert Ashton was born in Calcutta (now Kolkata), India. He first played for Essex in 1921 while he was a Cambridge student, and the following year he was named as one of *Wisden's* Cricketers of the Year. Later in 1922, however, he left England to work in India for an oil company, and did not play for the county again until 1927, when he returned on leave. Although he played only 21 matches for Essex, he was to have a huge role in the fortunes of the club when he later served as chairman and president. In 1943 he was appointed High Sheriff for the County of Essex and in 1950 he became Conservative MP for Chelmsford, holding the seat until 1964. He was knighted in 1959.

TUESDAY 14th FEBRUARY 1950

William Faviell died at the age of 67 in Nairobi, Kenya, having moved to Africa the previous year to live near his son. He was born in Loughton in 1882, and pursued a career in the army. He represented Essex in seven championship matches in the 1908 season, scoring 104 runs at 13 and bowling just five overs without taking a wicket. His military career proved to be more successful: he was present at the Gallipoli landings, and rose to become a lieutenant-colonel in the Worcestershire Regiment. In 1917 he was awarded the Distinguished Service Order and the Serbian Order of the White Eagle. From 1933 to 1945 he was Major and Resident Warden of the Tower of London, where a plaque in his honour can still be seen.

MONDAY 15th FEBRUARY 1993

Wicketkeeper-batsman Ben Foakes was born in Colchester. He played for the Essex second XI at the age of 15, and toured with the England Under-19 team in 2011. He made his first-class debut for Essex later in the same year against Sri Lanka.

FRIDAY 16th FEBRUARY 1923

Essex batsman Jack Russell batted throughout the first day of the final Test against South Africa in Durban. *Wisden* praised Russell for playing "splendid cricket of a defensive kind" and noted his strength through the leg-side. He ended the day 136 not out, although he would be dismissed on the following morning for the addition of four more runs. Russell would go on to create history in this game by becoming the first England batsman to record a century in both innings of a Test match.

THURSDAY 17th FEBRUARY 1921

Jack Leiper was born in Woodford Green. He played two matches for the county in 1950 as an opening bowler, but took only one wicket. He made a greater contribution with the bat, scoring 44 in an ultimately unsuccessful rearguard against Somerset at Bath, where he shared in a ninth-wicket stand of 79 with Trevor Bailey. His son, Robert, would also play for Essex and also manage just two appearances, in 1981 and 1982.

FRIDAY 18th FEBRUARY 1938

Barry Knight was born in Chesterfield, Derbyshire. He joined Essex from school and played 239 matches between 1955 and 1966, scoring 8,798 runs at 24.64 and taking 761 wickets at 22.55. In this period he established himself as one of England's leading all-rounders, and he played a total of 29 Tests, scoring two centuries. He left the county in 1967 after being passed over for the captaincy, and joined Leicestershire, later moving to Australia.

WEDNESDAY 18th FEBRUARY 1948

Bruce Francis was born in Sydney, Australia. He played two seasons for Essex as an overseas player, in 1971 and 1973, appearing in 47 matches, mostly as an opening batsman, and scoring 2,962 runs at an average of 38.46. In 1972 he was a member of the Australian tour party to England and played in three Test matches.

TUESDAY 19th FEBRUARY 1901

Claude Ashton was born in Calcutta (now Kolkata), India. He played 89 matches for Essex in the inter-war years, scoring 3,193 runs at 23.47, including three centuries, and taking 97 wickets at 30.13. His older brothers Hubert and Percy also played for the county, and a fourth brother, Gilbert, played for Worcestershire. Claude was a fine all-round sportsman and captained England at football against Northern Ireland in 1925. He became a flight lieutenant in the RAF during the Second World War, and was killed in a plane crash during a training mission in North Wales.

FRIDAY 20th FEBRUARY 1857

Former Essex captain Alfred "Bunny" Lucas was born in Westminster. He was noted for the correctness of his defensive play, and had played for Cambridge University, Surrey, and Middlesex, as well as appearing in five Tests for England, before he joined Essex in 1889. He scored 103 against MCC on his Essex debut, and captained the side from 1889 until 1894, the year in which the county achieved first-class status. He continued to play until 1907, when he was 50, appearing in 98 first-class matches for the county, in which he scored 3,554 runs at an average of 26.92, including two centuries.

TUESDAY 20th FEBRUARY 1923

Jack Russell completed his second century of the match for England against South Africa in Durban, becoming the first English player to achieve this feat. Most of the work had been done the previous day when he batted down the order because he was ill. Entering with England in trouble on 26 for 4, he helped to engineer a recovery, sharing half-century partnerships with Andy Sandham and — for the last wicket — with Arthur Gilligan, and he was unbeaten on 90 at stumps. On day four he completed his century and was finally dismissed for 111, by which time his side's lead had grown to 343. England eventually bowled the South Africans out for 234 to complete a series victory.

WEDNESDAY 21st FEBRUARY 1996

Ray Smith died in Kidderminster at the age of 81. He played 419 matches for Essex between 1934 and 1956, scoring 11,125 runs at 19.69 with six centuries, and taking 1,317 wickets at an average of 30.23. He played when the county's bowling resources were limited and often opened the bowling at medium pace and then returned to bowl off-breaks with the old ball. Yet he thrived on this workload, completing the double of 1,000 runs and 100 wickets for the county in both 1947 and 1950.

TUESDAY 22RD FEBRUARY 2011

Ryan ten Doeschate embarrassed the English team with a century for the Netherlands during a World Cup match in Nagpur. He hit 119 from 110 balls, including nine fours and three sixes, helping the Dutch post a highly competitive total of 292. England never looked completely at ease in their reply, but eventually reached their target with eight balls to spare thanks to a quickfire unbeaten 30 from ten Doeschate's Essex team-mate Ravi Bopara.

FRIDAY 23rd FEBRUARY 1934

Michael Bear was born in Brentwood. He played in 322 first-class matches for the county between 1954 and 1968, scoring 12,564 runs at an average of 24.25, including nine centuries. He was also widely regarded as one of the outstanding fielders of his generation.

TUESDAY 23th FEBRUARY 1937

Claude Buckenham died in Dundee aged 61. He played 258 matches for Essex between 1899 and 1914, taking 932 wickets at an average of 26.36, and also made 4,882 late-order runs, including two centuries. But for the notoriously poor catching of the Essex side he played in, his figures might well have been even more impressive. As it was, he was rated as one of the fastest bowlers of his generation and played in four Tests for England on the tour of South Africa in 1909, capturing 21 wickets at 28.23. After leaving Essex he played as a club professional in Scotland.

THURSDAY 24th FEBRUARY 1949

John Lever was born in Stepney. One of the great servants of Essex cricket, he played 443 first-class matches for the county between 1967 and 1989, taking 1,473 wickets at an average of 23.53. He spearheaded the county's attack in the championship-winning seasons of 1979, 1983, and 1984, taking over 100 wickets in each campaign. He also made 21 Test appearances for England, and was voted the Professional Cricketers' Association Player of the Year in 1978 and 1979.

SATURDAY 24th FEBRUARY 1990

Nasser Hussain made his Test debut in Kingston, Jamaica, against a West Indies side whose bowling attack contained Patrick Patterson, Ian Bishop, Malcolm Marshall, and Courtney Walsh. He did not get to bat on the opening day as England bowled out the West Indies for 164 and closed on 80-2. On the following day he came in at number six and scored 13. He was not required to bat again as England cruised to an unexpected victory by eight wickets.

TUESDAY 25th FEBRUARY 1964

Don Topley was born in Canterbury, Kent. He first came to public attention as a substitute fielder for England in 1984 when he was a member of the Lord's ground-staff. The following year he played a single match for Surrey before joining Essex, and went on to play 113 matches for the county, taking 336 wickets at 28.06. His son, Reece Topley, made his debut for Essex in 2011.

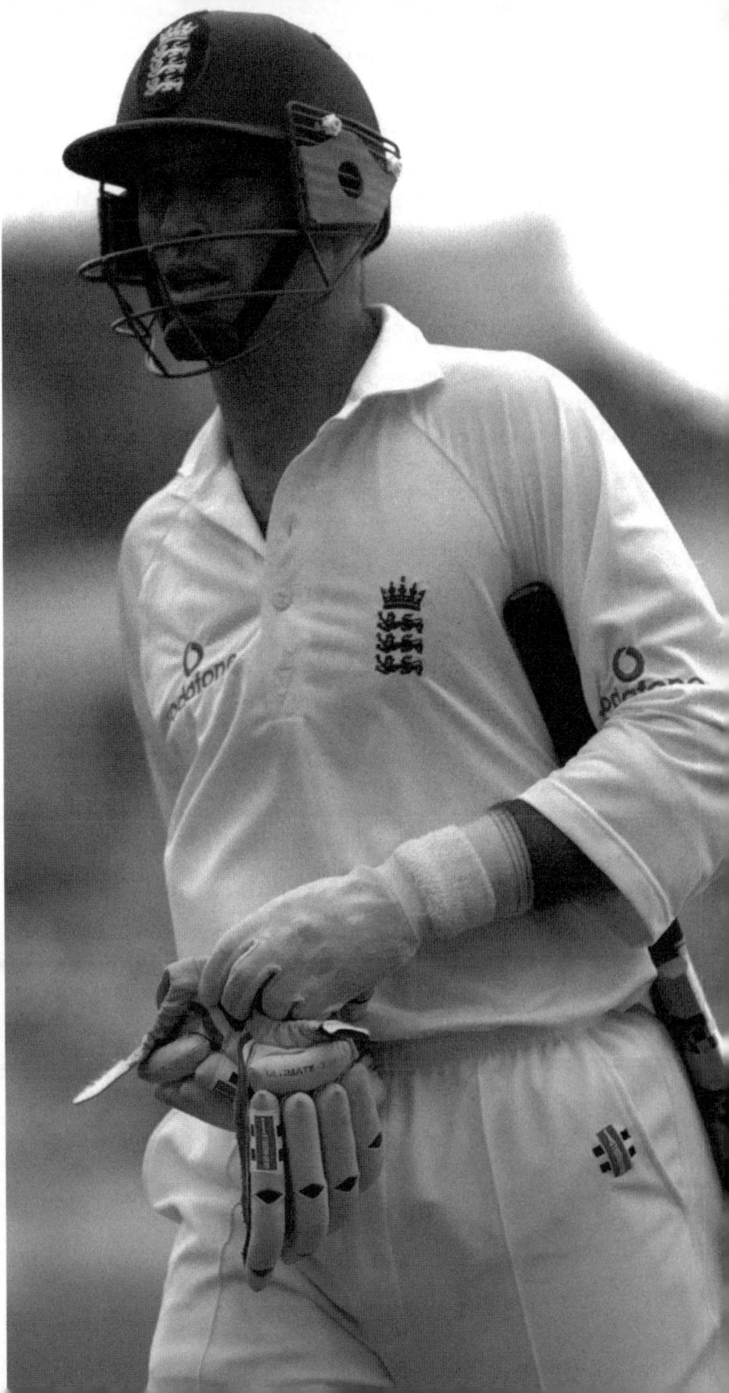

NASSER HUSSAIN MADE HIS TEST DEBUT IN FEBRUARY 1990

FRIDAY 26th FEBRUARY 1993

Former Essex player Allan Border became the leading scorer in Test match history, overtaking Sunil Gavaskar's total of 10,122 during an innings of 88 in the first Test against New Zealand at Christchurch. Border would retire the following year with an aggregate of 11,174, and held the record until 2005 when he was passed by Brian Lara.

WEDNESDAY 27th FEBRUARY 1895

Percy Ashton was born in Calcutta (now Kolkata), India. One of three brothers to play for Essex, he did not achieve the high standards of Hubert or Claude, but then he had the disadvantage of losing an eye after being gassed in the First World War. He was still good enough to play one match for Essex against Middlesex at Leyton in 1924 when he scored 31 and 21 and also took a wicket. He died in Bigbury-on-Sea, Devon, in 1934 at the age of 39.

FRIDAY 27th FEBRUARY 2009

Ravi Bopara recorded his first Test century while playing for England against the West Indies in Bridgetown, Barbados. His 104 came off 143 balls and included nine fours and a six, as he took advantage of being dropped when he had made only four. He shared in partnerships of 149 with Paul Collingwood and 113 with Tim Ambrose as England eventually declared on 600 for 6. However, the West Indies replied with a massive 749 for 9 and the match was drawn. Another Essex player, Alastair Cook, would score a century in England's second innings.

MONDAY 28th FEBRUARY 1944

Brian Ward was born in Chelmsford. An opening batsman, he played 128 first-class matches for the county between 1967 and 1972, scoring 4,799 runs at an average of 23.64, including four hundreds. He emigrated to Argentina in 1973, and represented his adopted country at the ICC Trophy in England in 1979.

ESSEX CCC
On This Day

MARCH

SUNDAY 1st MARCH 1992

Derek Pringle returned the remarkable bowling analysis of 8.2–5–8–3 during England's match against Pakistan at Adelaide during the opening phase of the World Cup. Pakistan were bowled out for just 74 in difficult conditions, with Pringle's Essex team-mate Saleem Malik top-scoring on 17. However, Pakistan escaped defeat when the game was abandoned due to rain. This no-result allowed them to scrape enough points to reach the semi-finals, and they would later turn the tables on England in the final, depriving Pringle and Graham Gooch of the chance to become world champions.

WEDNESDAY 1st MARCH 2006

Alastair Cook made his Test debut for England against India at Nagpur in unusual circumstances. He had been playing on England A's tour of the West Indies when Marcus Trescothick and Michael Vaughan had to drop out of the Test team, so Cook was flown halfway around the world and rushed into the side. He made the most of his opportunity, scoring 60 in his first innings and following this up with an unbeaten 104 in the second innings three days later.

FRIDAY 2nd MARCH 1973

Darren Robinson was born in Braintree. A solid opening batsman whose sturdy physique earned him the nickname "Pieshop", he played 136 first-class matches for the county between 1993 and 2003, scoring 7,149 runs at an average of 31.49, including 15 centuries, with a highest score of 200 against New Zealand in 1999. He left Essex to join Leicestershire in 2004.

MONDAY 3rd MARCH 2003

Neil Smith died of cancer in Dewsbury, Yorkshire, at the age of 53. As a young man he played eight matches for his native Yorkshire, but failed to win a regular place. He moved to Essex in 1973 and soon took over from Brian Taylor as the county's regular wicketkeeper. He played 178 first-class matches for the county, scoring 3,225 runs at an average of 18.01 and taking 380 catches and 47 stumpings, and was a regular member of the team that brought the county its first trophies in 1979.

MONDAY 4th MARCH 1912

Victor Evans was born in Woodford. An off-break and medium-pace bowler, he played 62 first-class matches for Essex between 1932 and 1937, taking 129 wickets at an average of 29.79. His best performance came against Gloucestershire at Southend in 1935, when he took ten wickets in the match as Essex won by 63 runs.

TUESDAY 4th MARCH 1986

Graham Gooch played one of his greatest one-day innings to carry England to a rare victory over the then-dominant West Indian side at Port-of-Spain, Trinidad. In a match shortened by rain to 37 overs, England looked anything but winners when Viv Richards smashed 82 from 39 balls to help the West Indies post an imposing total of 229. Gooch responded by hitting 129 not out from 118 balls, including 17 fours and a six. The magnitude of the innings can be gauged by the standard of the opposition bowlers: Garner, Patterson, Walsh, Marshall, and Harper. Only Wilf Slack with 34 provided any significant assistance, but Gooch saw England home by five wickets, scrambling a leg-bye off the last ball to seal the win.

MONDAY 5th MARCH 1906

Fast bowler Tom Smith was born in Warley. A banker by profession, he played 25 first-class matches for Essex as an amateur between 1929 and 1936, taking 63 wickets at an average of 27.61. His finest hour came against Middlesex at Lord's in 1929, when he clean bowled three batsmen in the space of four balls without conceding a run, one of the balls literally snapping the middle stump in two. His efforts were to no avail, however, as Essex lost by six wickets. He died in 1995 at the age of 89.

FRIDAY 6th MARCH 1914

Len Clark was born in Manor Park. He was already 32 when he made his debut for Essex in 1946. Over the next two seasons he played 24 matches for the county as a middle-order batsman, scoring 745 runs at an average of 18.17, with four half-centuries. His highest score was 64, made in a defeat to Northamptonshire at Ilford in 1947.

SATURDAY 7th MARCH 1914

Henry van Straubenzee was born in Johannesburg, South Africa. He played only one first-class match for the county, against Sussex in 1938, scoring four not out and bowling six overs without taking a wicket, as Essex won by an innings. He also played cricket for the army, in which he served as a lieutenant-colonel and won the Distinguished Service Order for his service as a tank commander in Italy during the Second World War. After a back injury curtailed his military career, he joined the firm of WH Smith and rose to become its managing director. He died in 2002 at the age of 88.

THURSDAY 8th MARCH 2001

Nasser Hussain played a captain's innings of 109 to help set up an England victory against Sri Lanka in the second Test in Kandy. After England had bowled out their hosts for 297 on the previous day, Hussain hit 12 fours and three sixes in a five-hour century, putting on 167 for the third wicket with Graham Thorpe as England built a first-innings lead of 90 and eventually won by three wickets.

THURSDAY 9th MARCH 1944

Lee Irvine was born in Durban, South Africa. He was the first overseas player to be signed by Essex following the relaxation of restrictions in 1967 when counties were allowed to sign one player without first establishing a residential qualification. Irvine, who had previously played for Natal, joined Essex in 1968 and played 54 first-class matches for the county over the next two seasons, scoring 2,674 runs at an average of 34.72, with a highest score of 109 against Glamorgan at Swansea in 1969.

WEDNESDAY 10th MARCH 1982

Future Essex player Saleem Malik hit an unbeaten century while making his debut for Pakistan against Sri Lanka in the first Test at Karachi. His 100 not out included ten fours. He was still a month short of his 19th birthday, and thus became the youngest player to score a Test century on debut. The innings put Pakistan into a strong position, and they won the game by 204 runs.

THURSDAY 11th MARCH 1976

David Thompson was born in Wandsworth. He made his first-class debut with Surrey in 1994, and toured the West Indies with England Under-19s the following year, in a squad that contained Andrew Flintoff and Marcus Trescothick. He failed to win a place in the Surrey team and played second-XI cricket for Lancashire before he joined Essex in 1999. Thompson played ten first-class matches for the county in 1999 and 2000, taking 26 wickets at an average of 30.42.

FRIDAY 12th MARCH 2010

Alastair Cook took favourably to the task of captaining England, hitting an unbeaten 158 against Bangladesh on the first day of his first series as skipper. Cook had been handed the captaincy on a temporary basis to fill in for the resting Andrew Strauss, and would lead his team to a 2-0 series win. He reached his 150 just before the close of the first day's play, scoring the runs from 222 balls, with 14 fours and two sixes. On the following day he would eventually be dismissed for 173 as England racked up 599 for 6 declared.

MONDAY 13th MARCH 1989

Tom Westley was born in Cambridge. He played for the Essex second XI as a 15-year-old and made his first-class debut for the county in 2006. By the end of the 2011 season he had played 41 matches for Essex, scoring 1,860 runs at 28.18, including two centuries.

SUNDAY 14th MARCH 1965

John Stephenson was born in Stebbing. He played 191 first-class matches for the county in two spells, firstly between 1985 and 1994 and then between 2002 and 2004. In these matches he scored 10,243 runs at an average of 35.68, including 17 centuries. He was also a useful medium-pace bowler, especially in one-day cricket. In between his two Essex stints he played seven seasons for Hampshire. Stephenson was selected for a single Test match, against Australia at The Oval in 1989, in which he opened the batting with his county colleague Graham Gooch and scored 25 and 11. He later served as head of cricket at MCC.

FRIDAY 15th MARCH 1991

George Eastman died in Eastbourne at the age of 87. Born in Leyton, he followed his older brother Laurie into the Essex team and kept wicket for the county in 48 first-class matches between 1926 and 1929, recording 29 catches and 21 stumpings. He was a confirmed number 11 batsman and scored his 261 runs at an average of just 6.86.

MONDAY 16th MARCH 1863

Arthur Johnston was born in Hornsey, Middlesex. He had played three matches for his native county before joining Essex in 1889, and was a regular opening batsman for the county club in the years just before it achieved first-class status. He appeared in only seven first-class matches for Essex, scoring an aggregate of 235 runs at 21.36, but he contributed to some notable achievements. Johnston was in the first Essex side to win a first-class match, against Oxford University at Leyton in 1894. Then in 1895 at Harrogate he made 63, the highest score of the match, as Essex, in their first season of County Championship cricket, pulled off a surprising victory over a powerful Yorkshire side.

FRIDAY 16th MARCH 1888

Fred Cooper was born in Wetherby, Yorkshire. He played ten first-class matches for the county between 1921 and 1923 as a medium-pace bowler, averaging 48.12, and fared little better with the bat, averaging just ten. However, he did manage a half-century against Gloucestershire at Leyton in 1921 and also had a five-wicket haul against the Combined Services in the following season.

MONDAY 17th MARCH 1884

Arthur Watson was born in Newdigate, Surrey. He played in two matches for Essex in the years before the First World War: against Derbyshire in 1913 he made 37 in the second innings as Essex held on for a draw; then against Leicestershire the following season he made 24 and 12 as Essex fell to a heavy defeat. After the war he had a long association with Sussex, playing 104 first-class matches for the south-coast county between 1922 and 1928. He died in Partridge Green, Sussex, in 1952 at the age of 77.

THURSDAY 18th MARCH 1954

Walter Mead, known as "the Essex Treasure", died in Ongar at the age of 85. The first great player to have played for Essex, he appeared in 332 first-class matches between 1894 and 1913, taking 1,472 wickets at an average of 19.30, including ten wickets in a match an astonishing 30 times. He also made one Test appearance for England against Australia in 1899. At his funeral, the minister expressed a wish that he would bowl on perfect pitches for eternity — a statement that drew some scorn from his surviving team-mates, who realised that, as a bowler who relied on extracting spin from the pitch, an imperfect surface would be much more attractive.

MONDAY 19th MARCH 1906

Norman "Tiger" Wykes was born in Woodford. He won a Blue at Cambridge and played 30 first-class matches for Essex between 1925 and 1936, scoring 879 runs at an average of 22.53, with one century, 162 against Kent at Leyton in 1927. His appearances for the county were limited by his duties as a schoolmaster at Eton.

MONDAY 20th MARCH 1972

Muneed Diwan was born in St Stephen in the Canadian province of New Brunswick. He played just one first-class match for Essex, in 1994, and it was not a happy occasion: he bagged a pair as his side lost to Leicestershire by an innings. He later represented Canada with some success in the ICC Trophy, helping them to seventh place in the tournament in Malaysia in 1997 and to third place on home soil in 2001.

SUNDAY 21st MARCH 1984

Allan Border played a match-saving innings for Australia in the second Test against the West Indies in Port-of-Spain. He had earlier been stranded on 98 not out in Australia's first innings as his side conceded a first-innings lead of 213. Australia began the last day staring defeat in the face on 53 for 3, but Border resisted for four and a half hours, receiving sterling support from last man Terry Alderman, and scored exactly 100 to secure the draw.

WEDNESDAY 22nd MARCH 1944

Bill Reeves died in Hammersmith at the age of 68. He was one of the great servants of the county in its early years in the County Championship, playing 271 matches between 1897 and 1921, taking 581 wickets at 27.77 and scoring 6,451 runs at an average of 16.62. He initially made his mark as a bowler, taking 106 wickets in the 1904 season. As his bowling declined, he became known as a powerful late-order hitter. He scored three centuries for the county, including a career-best 135 against Lancashire at Leyton in 1905. After retiring as a player he became an umpire and stood in five Test matches.

MONDAY 23rd MARCH 1885

Charles Stewart Richardson was born in Terling. He played just one first-class match for the county, against Yorkshire in 1914, and scored 15 in his only innings in a drawn game. He later served the club as chairman from 1928 to 1945. In 1947 he was elected president of the club, a post he held until his death the following year.

WEDNESDAY 24th MARCH 2010

Alastair Cook scored an unbeaten century to lead England to victory in the second Test match against Bangladesh at Mirpur. The home side had put up stubborn resistance before being bowled out on the last day, leaving England to chase 209 at over four runs per over. Cook responded with an innings of 109 from 156 balls and Kevin Pietersen contributed a brisk 74 as England eased to victory by nine wickets.

WEDNESDAY 25th MARCH 2009

Essex won the ProArch trophy, beating Middlesex in the final of the pre-season event in Abu Dhabi. They had won all three of their group matches in the eight-team tournament, and clinched victory in the final by five wickets with 13 balls to spare after restricting their opponents to 235 for 9 from their 50 overs. Matt Walker, who had signed from Kent in the off-season, guided Essex to victory with 77 not out from 97 balls, including six fours and a six, and was named man of the match.

ALASTAIR COOK HIT AN UNBEATEN CENTURY FOR ENGLAND IN MARCH 2010

WEDNESDAY 26th MARCH 1862

Harry Pickett was born in Stratford. He first played for Essex in the 1880s, before the county achieved first-class status. Nevertheless, he was still a regular member of the bowling attack in Essex's first years in the championship and played in 52 first-class matches, taking 114 wickets at 24.38. He still holds the record for the best bowling analysis by an Essex player with 10 for 32 against Leicestershire in 1895. After his playing career was over, he worked as a coach at Clifton College. He drowned in the sea off Aberavon in South Wales in 1907 at the age of 45.

SATURDAY 27th MARCH 1943

Eddie Presland was born in High Beech. He played 30 first-class matches for the county between 1962 and 1970, although his availability was limited by his other career as a professional footballer for West Ham United, Crystal Palace, and Colchester United. He made 625 runs at an average of 16.89 including just one half-century.

MONDAY 27th MARCH 2006

Neil Williams died of pneumonia at the age of 43. He was born in the Caribbean island of St Vincent and moved to England as a teenager. He played the bulk of his career for Middlesex, featuring in four championship-winning sides and appearing in a single Test for England against India at The Oval in 1990. Williams joined Essex in 1995 and played 33 first-class matches for the county over the next four seasons, taking 95 wickets at an average of 32.50.

THURSDAY 28th MARCH 1968

Former Essex and England captain Nasser Hussain was born in Madras (now Chennai), India. He made his Essex debut in 1987 and played 189 first-class matches for the county, scoring 11,982 runs at an average of 44.05, including 31 centuries, and he captained the side in 1999 and 2000. He played 96 Tests for England, scoring 14 centuries. As captain of England between 1999 and 2003 he was widely credited with instilling a more professional approach in the national side. Hussain retired from cricket in 2004 and became a television commentator on the sport.

TUESDAY 29th MARCH 1994

Essex's Mark Waugh teamed up with former Essex star Allan Border to save the third Test between Australia and South Africa at Durban. The pair came together on the last day with Australia four runs ahead and four wickets down, but they held firm for nearly four hours to bat out the game, Waugh ending undefeated on 113. At the end of the match Border announced his retirement after an illustrious Test career in which he had set new records for the most appearances (156), the most runs (11,174), and the most games as captain (93).

MONDAY 30th MARCH 1914

Frank Rist was born in Wandsworth. He played 65 first-class matches for the county between 1934 and 1953, often filling in as an emergency wicketkeeper. He scored 1,496 runs at an average of 15.11, but featured in some significant partnerships, and made 56 not out to save a match against Leicestershire in 1948. He later made an important contribution to the county by coaching and developing young players. He died in Whipps Cross in 2001 at the age of 87.

TUESDAY 30th MARCH 1954

Trevor Bailey produced his best Test bowling performance, taking 7 for 34 from 16 overs on the first day of the final Test between the West Indies and England at Kingston. The powerful West Indies line-up — which included Frank Worrell, Clyde Walcott and Everton Weekes, as well as a young Garry Sobers making his debut at number nine — was bowled out for 139 on an apparently good wicket, Bailey's victims including Jeff Stollmeyer and Weekes. They put up an improved showing second time around, but England still won by nine wickets.

FRIDAY 30th MARCH 1990

Jaik Mickleburgh was born in Norwich. He made his debut for Essex in 2008 and established himself as a fixture in the county's middle-order in 2010. By the end of the 2011 season he had played 41 first-class matches, scoring 2,080 runs at an average of 27.36, including a top score of 174 against Durham at Chester-le-Street in 2010.

SATURDAY 31st MARCH 1900

Steriker Norman Hare was born in Tottenham. He made a spectacular debut for Essex against Derbyshire in 1921, coming in at number ten and hitting 98 in a record ninth-wicket partnership with Johnny Douglas. However, his appearances were limited by his business commitments with the Anglo-Persian Oil Company. He played in only two further games, making a pair against Somerset in his final appearance. In later life he received the CBE for his services to business. He died at Meadle, Buckinghamshire, in 1977.

WEDNESDAY 31st MARCH 1971

Paul Grayson was born in Ripon, Yorkshire. He joined Essex in 1996 after six seasons with Yorkshire and played 128 first-class matches for the county between then and 2004, scoring 6,589 runs at an average of 32.78, including 15 centuries, and taking 123 wickets at 42.21. After retiring from first-team cricket he led Essex's second XI, and in 2007 he became head coach. In 2009 he led the side to promotion to the first division of the County Championship.

ESSEX CCC
On This Day

APRIL

WEDNESDAY 1st APRIL 1953

Frank Gillingham died in Monaco at the age of 77. He was born in Tokyo, Japan, and educated at Dulwich College and Durham University. He was a serving curate in Leyton when he first played for Essex in 1903. Although his duties as a clergyman prevented him from appearing regularly, Gillingham continued to play until 1928, aged 52, and holds the distinction of being the oldest player to represent Essex. In 181 matches he scored 9,160 runs at 32.02 with 19 centuries. He also provided the first ever radio commentary on a match, when Essex played the touring New Zealanders in 1927. In 1939 he became chaplain to King George VI, and he later served as chaplain to Queen Elizabeth II.

FRIDAY 2nd APRIL 1875

Frederick Bull was born in Hackney. He was an off-break bowler who played 88 first-class matches for the county between 1895 and 1900, taking 365 wickets at an average of 21.75, including ten wickets in a match on five occasions. In 1898 he became the first Essex player to be named as one of *Wisden's* Cricketers of the Year, but a couple of years later he had become ineffective and lost his place in the Essex side. He drowned himself in 1910 at the age of 35.

MONDAY 2nd APRIL 1917

Edward Coleman died at the age of 27 in Salonica (now Thessaloniki) in Greece, where he was serving as a lieutenant in the East Anglian Regiment. He was born in Southend and played two first-class matches as a wicketkeeper for Essex in 1912, taking one catch and one stumping, and scoring ten runs in three innings.

TUESDAY 2nd APRIL 1935

Geoff Smith was born in Braintree. He was an opening batsman who played 239 first-class matches for Essex between 1955 and 1966, scoring 8,519 runs at 22.30 and taking 33 wickets with his off-breaks at 27.66. He passed 1,000 runs in a season four times and hit four centuries, with a highest score of 148 against Derbyshire at Chelmsford in 1961. He later played Minor Counties cricket for Hertfordshire.

SATURDAY 3rd APRIL 1869

John Bonner was born in Mile End. He played 16 first-class matches for the county between 1896 and 1898, scoring 339 runs at 13.03, with a top score of 59 in a victory over Derbyshire at Derby in 1896. He died in Bournemouth in 1936 at the age of 67.

SATURDAY 4th APRIL 1981

John Maunders was born in Ashford, Middlesex. He joined Essex in 2008 after spells with Middlesex and Leicestershire and played 21 first-class matches for the county over the next three seasons, scoring 1,145 runs at 32.71 and taking 24 wickets at an average of 38.66. He hit three centuries for Essex, with a top score of 150 against his old team Leicestershire in 2009.

TUESDAY 5th APRIL 1938

Tony Stanyard was born in Plaistow. He played a number of matches for the Essex second XI in the latter half of the 1950s, but only appeared in two first-class matches for the county, the home games against Kent and South Africa at Ilford in 1960. He scored 26 in the drawn game against Kent, and followed this with seven and 14 in the loss to the South Africans.

WEDNESDAY 6th APRIL 1842

Essex's first captain, James Round, was born in Colchester. He was educated at Eton and Oxford University and was rated as one of the best amateur wicketkeepers of his day. He played 22 first-class matches for Oxford and MCC between 1864 and 1869, scoring 472 runs at 16.85 and claiming 20 catches and 14 stumpings. He also appeared in non-first-class cricket for numerous teams, including the Gentlemen of Essex. Round was elected Member of Parliament for East Essex in 1868 and served various constituencies in the county until 1906. In 1876 he organised and chaired the meeting that formed the Essex County Cricket Club. He was elected the club's chairman, treasurer, and captain, and appeared in some of the earliest matches. He relinquished the captaincy in 1882, giving way to Charles Green. He died in 1916 at his home, Birch Hall, at the age of 74.

WEDNESDAY 6th APRIL 1898

Charlie Bray was born in Brighton. He played 95 first-class matches for Essex as an amateur between 1927 and 1937, scoring 3,474 runs at an average of 24.81, including five centuries. He also stood in as captain when Johnny Douglas and Whiz Morris were unavailable. Bray was a professional journalist, working principally with the *Daily Herald*, and wrote a history of Essex cricket which was published in 1950. He died in Bedford in 1993 at the age of 95.

TUESDAY 7th APRIL 1914

Brian Belle was born in Woodford Green. He played 26 matches for Essex between 1935 and 1937 while he was a student at Oxford University. He scored 776 runs for the county at an average of 19.89, with a highest score of 63 against Yorkshire at Huddersfield in 1935. In that game Belle shared in a partnership of 174 runs for the sixth wicket with Stan Nichols as Essex defeated the strong Yorkshire side by an innings. He gave up first-class cricket to pursue a teaching career, and later captained Suffolk. He died in Campsea Ash, Suffolk, in 2007 at the age of 92.

WEDNESDAY 8th APRIL 1922

Cunliffe Gosling died at Hassobury, his family's country house on the Essex-Hertfordshire border, aged 63. He had played for Cambridge University and then appeared in four first-class matches for Essex between 1894 and 1896, scoring 55 runs at 7.85. However, Gosling was better known as a footballer, playing for the Old Etonians and winning five caps for England between 1892 and 1895, the last as captain. He also served as High Sheriff for the County of Essex in 1902.

THURSDAY 9th APRIL 1970

Stan Quin died in Bishops Glen, near Bloemfontein, in South Africa, at the age of 74. He played one first-class match for Essex, against Middlesex at Lord's in 1924. The match was ruined by rain, and Quin bowled seven overs without taking a wicket and scored a duck in his only innings. He later played two Currie Cup matches for his native Orange Free State.

FRIDAY 10th APRIL 1981

Graham Gooch scored 153 on the first day of the final Test between England and the West Indies at Kingston, his second century of the series. Gooch topped the England batting averages with 460 runs at 57.50, establishing himself as a player of true international class. Despite Gooch's effort, England were bowled out for 285 and conceded a large first-innings lead, but they saved the match thanks to a century in the second innings from David Gower.

SUNDAY 11th APRIL 2004

James Middlebrook reached his maiden first-class century in Essex's match against Cambridge University at Fenner's. His unbeaten 101 was scored from 139 balls and included eight fours and four sixes as the county enjoyed some early-season batting practice against the students. The innings came at the start of Middlebrook's second season for Essex and six years after he first played county cricket for Yorkshire.

FRIDAY 12th APRIL 1895

Orme Bristowe was born in Watford. He played 11 first-class matches for Essex while he was still a teenager in the years immediately before the First World War, and also played for Oxford University. He scored 249 runs for Essex at 16.60 and took 22 wickets with his leg-breaks at 40.95. Bristowe's highest score of 81 came against Leicestershire at Leyton in 1914 when he put on 78 for the last wicket with Bert Tremlin. After the war he devoted himself to golf and represented Great Britain in the 1924 Walker Cup. He died of heart failure at the age of 43.

SUNDAY 12th APRIL 1936

Bert Tremlin died in Woodford at the age of 58. He played 132 first-class matches for Essex between 1900 and 1919, taking 467 wickets at 25.82 and four times taking ten in a match. He also scored 1,776 runs at 13.66. He first became established in the side when Walter Mead was in dispute with the club in 1904 and 1905, but after Mead's return in 1906 his opportunities were limited. Only between 1910 and 1914 did he play regularly again.

WEDNESDAY 13th APRIL 1921

Harold Mead died in Bell Common at the age of 25. He was born in Walthamstow in 1895, the son of the great Essex bowler Walter Mead. He played alongside his father in two matches in 1913 — his father's last season — and also played twice in 1914, but took only three first-class wickets at an average of 64.66. In the First World War he served as a private in the Essex Regiment. He was seriously wounded in 1915 and died as a result of his injuries six years later.

THURSDAY 14th APRIL 1977

Gordon Melluish died in Little Bushey, Hertfordshire, at the age of 70. He was a slow left-arm bowler who played four first-class matches for Essex in 1926, taking three wickets at an average of 38.33 and scoring 18 runs at an average of nine. He had a long career as a club cricketer, playing over 300 matches for MCC and he also turned out for Northamptonshire in wartime matches.

TUESDAY 15th APRIL 1980

Essex captain and wicketkeeper James Foster was born in Whipps Cross. He made his debut against Glamorgan at Southend in 2000 and by the end of the 2011 season had played 165 first-class matches for the club, scoring 8,391 runs at 37.62 (with 14 centuries) and taking 467 catches and 42 stumpings. Foster has also played in seven Tests and represented England in one-day internationals and Twenty20 matches. He took over from Mark Pettini as county captain during the 2010 season.

TUESDAY 16th APRIL 1963

Saleem Malik was born in Lahore, Pakistan. He played 39 first-class matches for Essex in 1991 and 1993, scoring 2,889 runs at 55.55, including eight centuries, with a highest score of 215 against Leicestershire in 1991. He also took 39 wickets for the county at 32.43. Malik had a long Test career for Pakistan, appearing in 103 matches — 12 as captain — and scoring 5,768 runs at 43.69. In 2001 he was banned from cricket after an investigation into bribery allegations, but the punishment was lifted in 2008.

FRIDAY 16th APRIL 2010

Jaik Mickleburgh and James Foster put on a county-record partnership of 339 for the fifth wicket in the first innings against Durham at Chester-le-Street. The pair had come together on the previous day with the score 102 for 4 and they batted for over 100 overs before Mickleburgh was bowled by Liam Plunkett for 174. Foster was dismissed for 169 in the following over as Essex lost their last six wickets for 43 runs. Durham were forced to follow on, but batted out the last day to save the game.

THURSDAY 17th APRIL 1941

Laurie Eastman died in Harefield Hospital as a result of injuries sustained in an air raid. He was 43 and had been serving as an air raid warden during the London Blitz. He was born in Enfield Wash, Middlesex, in 1897 and saw action in the First World War, winning the Distinguished Service Medal and the Military Medal. Eastman played 442 first-class matches for Essex between 1920 and 1939, scoring 12,965 runs at 20.57 and taking 975 wickets at an average of 26.77. He passed 1,000 runs in a season five times and hit seven centuries, with a highest score of 161 against Derbyshire in 1929. He bowled both medium pace and leg spin, with best figures of 7 for 28 in a match-winning spell against Somerset in 1922. Eastman also served the club as assistant secretary, and was acting secretary in 1925.

SUNDAY 18th APRIL 1926

Doug Insole was born in Clapton. He played 345 first-class matches for Essex between 1947 and 1963, scoring 20,113 runs at an average of 38.67 including 48 centuries. He also kept wicket on occasion and was a useful medium-pace bowler, taking 119 wickets for the county at 34.12. His highest score was 219 not out against Yorkshire at Colchester in 1949. Insole captained the county side between 1950 and 1960 and was one of *Wisden's* Cricketers of the Year in 1956. He played nine Tests for England and later became a Test selector, England tour manager, and chairman of the Test and County Cricket Board. He has served Essex County Cricket Club as chairman and president and became a CBE in 1979.

WEDNESDAY 19th APRIL 1978

A 19-year-old Derek Pringle marked his debut for Essex with an unbeaten 50 against Cambridge University at Fenner's as the county totalled 351 for 4. The following year Pringle would appear in the corresponding fixture as a Cambridge player. He played for the university for four seasons, and in 1982 he became the last Cambridge player to play Test cricket while still an undergraduate.

WEDNESDAY 20th APRIL 1938

Derek Semmence was born in East Worthing, Sussex. He played most of his first-class matches for Sussex and was the youngest player to score a century for that county. His one appearance for Essex came in a match against Oxford University at The Parks in 1962, in which he scored 24 and nine and bowled eight overs without taking a wicket. He later played for Devon, Northumberland, and Cambridgeshire.

WEDNESDAY 21st APRIL 1909

Hubert Thorn was born in Tiptree. He played one first-class match for the county against Northamptonshire at Leyton in 1928. He scored five and seven and took 1 for 42 as Essex were routed by an innings. Thorn had a somewhat longer career as a London solicitor and died in Colchester in 1982 at the age of 73.

MONDAY 22nd APRIL 1901

Norman Saint was born in Islington. He played 44 first-class matches for Essex between 1920 and 1923, scoring 757 runs at 11.64 and taking 17 wickets at 47.05. He died in Whitechapel in 1930 at the age of only 29.

SATURDAY 22nd APRIL 1978

David Masters was born in Chatham, Kent. He made his first-class debut for Kent in 2000 and also played for Leicestershire before joining Essex in 2008. By the close of the 2011 season he had played in 59 first-class matches for the county and taken 233 wickets at 21.89 while also scoring 1,078 runs at 14.97. The 2011 season was his best to date: he was the leading wicket-taker in the County Championship with 93 at 18.13.

WEDNESDAY 23rd APRIL 1969

Nadeem Shahid was born in Karachi, Pakistan. He first came to prominence as a pupil at Ipswich School and was named the leading all-rounder in English schools cricket in 1988. He made his debut in 1989 and played 65 first-class matches for the county, scoring 2,523 runs at 31.14 (with two centuries) and taking 27 wickets at an average of 38.51. Shahid's highest score was 132, made in an innings victory over Kent at Chelmsford in 1992. After the 1994 season he moved to Surrey and played a further ten seasons at The Oval.

SATURDAY 23rd APRIL 1988

Graham Gooch achieved his highest score for the county, 275 against Kent. The match was the first four-day game ever played by Essex following a shake-up of the County Championship format. Kent had batted first and declared on 400 for 7, but Gooch's innings took Essex well past that mark. He shared partnerships of 259 with Derek Pringle and 154 with Keith Fletcher as Essex reached 616. Kent would bat late into the final day and set Essex a target of 169 from 25 overs, which they achieved thanks to a rapid 73 from Gooch.

FRIDAY 24th APRIL 1981

Umpires Nigel Plews and Don Oslear took the players off for an early lunch on the final day of Essex's season-opener against Cambridge University at Fenner's. The reason had nothing to do with rain or bad light, but rather involved the bitter northerly wind sweeping across the ground. The umpires justified their unprecedented actions by saying they considered it "unreasonable and dangerous to continue because of the extreme cold".

THURSDAY 25th APRIL 1991

John Stephenson hit his highest one-day score of 142 as Essex ran up 307 for 4 from their 55 overs against Warwickshire in the Benson and Hedges Cup. Stephenson and Saleem Malik (72) put on 170 for the third wicket, with Warwickshire's South African bowler Allan Donald going for more than seven an over. Dermot Reeve hit 80 in Warwickshire's reply, but Essex still won by 12 runs.

SATURDAY 26th APRIL 2003

Essex's match against Warwickshire at Edgbaston was tied after the county had been set a target of 380 by their hosts. Essex started the chase well, with half-centuries from Darren Robinson and Andy Flower, while Ronnie Irani hit 87 from 91 balls. However, Irani was sixth out with 80 still needed. Useful contributions followed from James Foster and Jonathan Dakin before James Middlebrook and Graham Napier reached the last over with only three runs required and two wickets in hand. Napier scored a single off the first ball, but then Middlebrook was given out leg-before-wicket to Ashley Giles. Last man Scott Brant came in and managed a single to level the scores, but Giles bowled Napier with his fifth ball to finish the match.

TUESDAY 27th APRIL 1875

Frederick Fane was born in Curragh Camp, County Kildare, in Ireland, where his father was serving in the British Army. He played 292 first-class matches for Essex between 1895 and 1922, scoring 12,599 runs at an average of 26.13, including 18 centuries. He was the first player to score a double-century for Essex and had a top score of 217 against Surrey at The Oval in 1911. He succeeded Charles Kortright as captain of Essex in 1904 and led the county for three seasons. Fane also played 14 Test matches and was the first Essex player to captain England. His cricket career petered out after the First World War, in which he gained the rank of captain and was awarded the Military Cross. He died in Brentwood in 1960 at the age of 85.

SUNDAY 27th APRIL 1969

Essex won their first match in the newly established Player's County League (later called the John Player League), beating Nottinghamshire by 37 runs at Chelmsford. They batted first and recovered from 67 for 6 to reach 185 for 9, thanks to 45 from Brian Edmeades and 48 from Stuart Turner. They then bowled out the visitors for 148, with Edmeades taking three wickets and three Nottinghamshire players being run out. The county would go on to enjoy a successful season in the new Sunday competition, finishing in third place with 11 wins and four defeats.

SUNDAY 28th APRIL 1968

Andy Flower was born in Cape Town, South Africa. He played Test cricket for Zimbabwe between 1992 and 2002 and averaged 51.54 over 63 matches. He joined Essex in 2002 and played 81 first-class matches for the county, scoring 6,215 runs at an average of 54.51 with 18 centuries and a top score of 271 not out against Northamptonshire in 2006. Flower retired in 2007 to become an assistant coach to the England team, and he succeeded Peter Moores as England team coach in 2009. He presided over the recovery of the Ashes in his first year, and in 2011 took England to the number one position in the world rankings following crushing series victories over both Australia and India.

FRIDAY 29th APRIL 2005

New Zealander Andre Adams took a hat-trick for Essex against Somerset on the third day of their match at Taunton. He had Michael Burns caught behind and then trapped Sanath Jayasuriya and James Hildreth leg-before-wicket to leave Somerset — who trailed by 237 after the first innings — in disarray on 65 for 4. Some late-order hitting on the following day forced Essex to bat again, but could not prevent a comfortable nine-wicket victory for the visitors. Adams was in his second season with Essex, and left after the following campaign to join Nottinghamshire, where he was the leading wicket-taker in the county's title-winning season of 2010.

MONDAY 30th APRIL 1906

Harry Crabtree was born in Barnoldswick, Yorkshire. He played two first-class matches for Essex in 1931, and then 22 matches in 1946 and 1947, scoring 1,281 runs at an average of 32.02. He made four centuries, with a top score of 146 against Nottinghamshire in 1946. He was a schoolteacher by profession, and took a leading role in the coaching of young cricketers around the county for many years. Crabtree's methods were highly successful, and he was appointed as a coaching advisor to MCC. He died at Great Baddow in 1982 at the age of 76.

ESSEX CCC
On This Day

MAY

FRIDAY 1st MAY 1908

Charles Crawley was born in Brandon, Suffolk. He played only one first-class match for Essex, against Leicestershire in 1929. In this match he had the opportunity to open the batting with his brother Leonard Crawley, who had already been playing for the county for three years. Charles was outshone by his brother in both innings, making a duck and three, while Leonard scored 58 and 47. Leonard would continue to play for Essex until 1936 — the year after Charles died in Sunderland at the age of just 27.

SUNDAY 2nd MAY 1976

Essex scored a resounding victory over Warwickshire in the John Player League at Ilford. Ken McEwan scored his first limited-overs matches and ended up with 123, putting on 133 for the third wicket with Keith Fletcher as Essex ran up 275 for 9 in their 40 overs. The visitors were never in the hunt and were bowled out for 148, with Brian Edmeades taking 3 for 29 and Graham Gooch 2 for 16, as Essex won by 127 runs.

THURSDAY 3rd MAY 1945

Sadiq Mohammad was born in Junagadh, in the Indian state of Gujarat — although he would play 41 Tests for Pakistan. He played county cricket for Gloucestershire from 1972 to 1982, but before that he turned out for Essex in one match in August 1970. This was against a touring Jamaica side, and the county took the opportunity to play three debutants in addition to Sadiq. Unfortunately, it did not turn out to be much of a match, with rain preventing any play on the first and last days. Sadiq scored 20 in his only innings.

SATURDAY 4th MAY 1968

Robin Hobbs took a hat-trick for Essex in the Gillette Cup first round match against Middlesex. Hobbs had not bowled at all in the innings before he was introduced for the last of the 60 overs. Up until this point Middlesex had been restricted to 150 for 7, but Hobbs' first three balls went for 11 runs. He then dismissed Hooker, Price, and Herman to end the innings.

TUESDAY 4th MAY 1971

Stuart Turner took a hat-trick for Essex on the last day of a drawn match against Surrey at The Oval. His victims were Storey, Long, and Jackman, but the excitement was diminished as the wickets were spread over two overs. Turner's effort left Surrey 226 ahead with only two wickets left, but they put on a further 31 runs and then had Essex in some trouble at 111 for 7 before Bruce Francis and Ray East batted out time.

SATURDAY 4th MAY 1985

Ravi Bopara was born in Forest Gate. He made his first-class debut for Essex as a 17-year-old against Northamptonshire in 2002. By the end of the 2011 season he had played 90 first-class matches for the county, scoring 5,933 runs at an average of 45.29, with 16 centuries and a highest score of 229 against Northamptonshire at Chelmsford in 2007. He is also the only player to have scored a double-century for Essex in a limited-overs match. In addition to his batting, Bopara has also taken 108 first-class wickets at an average of 41.12, with a best performance of 5 for 75 against Surrey in 2006. He was named the Cricket Writers' Club Young Cricketer of the Year in 2008, and in 2009 scored centuries for England in three consecutive Tests.

SATURDAY 5th MAY 1990

Graham Gooch and Paul Prichard established a new Essex record, taking their second-wicket partnership to 403 on the third day of the match against Leicestershire at Chelmsford. The partnership still stands as the highest for any wicket for the county. The pair had come together the previous day with Essex on 82 for 1 in reply to Leicestershire's total of 520 and still having plenty of work to do to save the follow-on. At the start of the third day the partnership stood at 76, and a further 327 runs were added before Gooch was dismissed for 215, including a six and 28 fours. Prichard went on to reach a career-best score of 245, with two sixes and 31 fours. Further contributions from Mark Waugh, Brian Hardie, and Neil Foster took the Essex score to 712 for 5 at the close of play.

SUNDAY 6th MAY 1962

Neil Foster was born in Colchester. He played 180 first-class matches as a pace bowler between 1980 and 1993, taking 747 wickets at an average of 23.59, with a best performance of 8 for 99 against Lancashire in 1991. He also scored 3,440 runs at an average of 22.05 with two centuries. Foster played 29 Tests for England, taking 88 wickets at 32.85, and was one of *Wisden's* Cricketers of the Year in 1988, but suffered persistent knee and back injuries in the course of his career and was forced to retire at the age of 31. He later qualified and practised as a physiotherapist.

FRIDAY 6th MAY 2011

Graham Napier took a hat-trick in Essex's Clydesdale Bank 40 match against Glamorgan. Glamorgan had made an excellent start to their innings with 116 for the first wicket before Napier broke the partnership when he had Gareth Rees caught behind. He then dismissed James Allenby and Stewart Walters, trapping both men leg-before-wicket with in-swinging yorkers, to complete the hat-trick. Napier finished the innings with figures of 4 for 38 from eight overs as Glamorgan were restricted to 222 for 7. However, rain intervened before Essex could begin their innings and the match was abandoned.

SATURDAY 7th MAY 1949

Essex found themselves on the wrong end of an extraordinary batting performance on the opening day of their match against Cambridge University at Fenner's. Cambridge batsmen John Dewes and Hubert Doggart put on 429 runs to establish a new record second-wicket partnership for English cricket. The stand was still unbroken at the close of play when the declaration was made, with Dewes not out on 204 and Doggart on 219. The chief Essex bowlers to suffer were Trevor Bailey, Ray Smith, and Eric Price, and it was a dispiriting introduction to first-class cricket for 16-year-old wicketkeeper Brian Taylor, who made his Essex debut in this match. Essex eventually salvaged a draw in benign batting conditions — not that a loss to this Cambridge side would amount to a disgrace: Dewes had already played for England, while Doggart scored over 2,000 runs that season and would go on to play two Tests himself.

WEDNESDAY 7th MAY 1975

Ashley Cowan was born in Hitchin, Hertfordshire. He played 102 first-class matches for Essex as a seam bowler between 1995 and 2005, taking 280 wickets at 32.26. His best performance came in 1999 with 6 for 47 against Glamorgan at Cardiff, while in 1996 he took a hat-trick against Gloucestershire. Cowan was also a useful late-order batsman, scoring 2,231 runs at 17.84 with a top score of 94 against Leicestershire at Grace Road in 1998 when he and Peter Such put on 102 for the last wicket. He reached the verge of the England team and was in the party that toured the West Indies in 1998, but never played a Test.

MONDAY 7th MAY 1990

Essex took their first-innings total to 761 for 6 — the highest in the county's history — before declaring against Leicestershire. The score was compiled in response to Leicestershire's 520 and featured a record stand of 403 between Graham Gooch and Paul Prichard on the Saturday. The final day began with Essex 192 ahead on 712 for 5, and the county batted on, giving Neil Foster, who resumed on 83 not out, the chance to score his maiden first-class century. Foster duly reached three figures, and was eventually run out for 101, with five sixes and eight fours. There was no opportunity for Essex to force a victory on a perfect pitch, and Leicestershire easily batted out the rest of the match, reaching 249 for 3.

FRIDAY 8th MAY 1942

Robin Hobbs was born in Chippenham in Wiltshire. A leg-spin bowler and useful lower-order batsman, he played 325 first-class matches for Essex between 1961 and 1975, taking 763 wickets at 26.00 and scoring 4,069 runs at 12.44. His best bowling figures were 8 for 63 against Glamorgan in 1966. He hit two centuries in his career — both scores of exactly 100 — including one from just 46 balls against Australia in 1975. He was the only established leg-spinner in England in the latter part of his career, and was selected to play in seven Tests. After leaving Essex he played for Suffolk and then returned to the first-class game to captain Glamorgan in 1979.

THURSDAY 8th MAY 1975

Keith Boyce produced a brilliant all-round performance on the second day against Leicestershire at Chelmsford. He came in with the score at 107 for 3 and hit a century in just 58 minutes with eight sixes and seven fours. He was eventually out for 113, having scored all but nine of the 122 runs added for the fourth wicket with Keith Fletcher. After Essex were all out for 300, Boyce took the new ball and dismissed two batsmen without a run on the board. Three further wickets followed, and Leicestershire closed on 60 for 9, Boyce having taken 5 for 25 from 13 overs. His excellent form continued the next day, and he finished with match figures of 12 for 73, although a century from Chris Balderstone allowed Leicestershire to escape with a draw.

TUESDAY 9th MAY 1923

Johnny Douglas became the first Essex player to take a hat-trick for the county twice. Eighteen years after he first performed the feat against Yorkshire, the 40-year-old captain did it again against Sussex at Leyton. He dismissed Maurice Tate for 97 to break a second-wicket partnership of 178 then had Ted Bowley — who had been Tate's partner in that stand — adjudged leg-before-wicket for 75 and bowled Thomas Cook for a duck. Douglas finished with 7 for 110 from 19 overs as Sussex were bowled out for 252. However, Essex were deep in trouble at 109 for 7 at the close. Douglas took a further five wickets in the second innings, but Essex lost the match by 290 runs.

TUESDAY 10th MAY 1892

Cyril Buxton died at the age of 26. He was born in Woodford Wells in 1865 and educated at Harrow and Cambridge University, where he played 30 first-class matches between 1885 and 1888. He first played for Essex in 1883, and was persuaded to remain with the county by Charles Green, even though it did not yet enjoy first-class status. In 1889 Buxton shared the club captaincy with Bunny Lucas, and he often deputised for Lucas in the following two seasons. He played his final game for the county in August 1891. He committed suicide the following year while suffering from severe depression.

THURSDAY 10th MAY 1962

Chris Gladwin was born in East Ham. He played 67 first-class matches for the county between 1981 and 1987, mainly as an opening batsman, scoring 2,953 runs at an average of 27.59. His only century was a score of 162 against Cambridge University in 1984. Gladwin later played four matches for Derbyshire in 1989. After retiring he became a respected coach in the Essex area.

FRIDAY 11th MAY 1888

Kenneth Gibson was born in Kensington. He was a talented amateur wicketkeeper who played 36 first-class matches for the county between 1909 and 1912, scoring 795 runs at an average of 16.22 with 53 catches and nine stumpings. His father — a former president of the Law Society — was created a baronet in 1925, and Kenneth succeeded to the title in 1932 as 2nd Baronet Gibson of Great Warley. He died in 1967 at the age of 79.

SUNDAY 11th MAY 2008

Essex racked up 391 for 5 in 50 overs — their highest total in one-day matches — in the Friends Provident Trophy group match against Surrey at The Oval. The foundation of the score was an opening stand of 269 between skipper Mark Pettini (who made his highest limited-overs score of 144, including 17 fours and two sixes) and Jason Gallian (117, with 15 fours). Acceleration was provided at the end of the innings by Ryan ten Doeschate (60 in 31 balls, including five fours and two sixes), and James Foster (46 in 23 balls, including a four and three sixes). The chief victim among the Surrey bowlers was Jade Dernbach, whose ten overs cost 107 runs. David Masters then took 5 for 17 as Surrey collapsed from 189 for 3 to 235 all out, leaving Essex winners by 156 runs.

THURSDAY 12th MAY 1921

Cyril Searle was born in Battersea. He played only one first-class match for Essex, keeping wicket against Cambridge University at Fenner's in 1947. He took one catch and scored five not out in his only innings. He died in Wandsworth in 2005 at the age of 83.

SATURDAY 13th MAY 1899

Essex scored a famous victory over Australia at Leyton. The tourists needed 200 to win on the last day, but Walter Mead and Sailor Young bowled unchanged on a pitch that offered considerable spin to dismiss them for only 73. Mead took 3 for 32 and Young 7 for 32. Both men would be picked for England in the coming summer.

FRIDAY 13th MAY 1977

James Middlebrook was born in Leeds. He played for Yorkshire for four seasons before joining Essex in 2002. He played 120 first-class matches for the county before leaving to join Northamptonshire after the 2009 season. An off-spinning all-rounder, Middlebrook scored 3,920 runs at 26.84, including four centuries, and took 270 wickets at an average of 40.19. He was also a valuable performer in one-day matches, forming an efficient spin partnership with Danish Kaneria.

FRIDAY 13th MAY 1994

Graham Gooch and Paul Prichard established a first-wicket record partnership for Essex, adding 316 in the first innings of the match against Kent. Gooch was the dominant partner, outscoring Prichard by two to one. The stand was eventually broken when Prichard was caught and bowled by Carl Hooper for 109. By this stage Essex had already built a lead of 125. Gooch went on to reach 236, with 28 fours and three sixes, as Essex reached 541 for 5 to set up a four-wicket victory.

MONDAY 14th MAY 1894

The club played its inaugural first-class match, against Leicestershire at Leyton. The move to first-class status had been approved by MCC the previous month, with Leicestershire, Warwickshire, and Derbyshire all similarly upgraded. Charles Kortright had the honour of bowling the first ball for the county, but the leading role was taken by Walter Mead, who took 6 for 49 as the visitors were all out for 131. However, any euphoria soon evaporated when Essex batted: they were all out for 57, with only Bob Carpenter reaching double figures, and Leicestershire were batting again by the close. Essex would put up a better show in their second innings, but still lost by 68 runs.

TUESDAY 14th MAY 1946

A thrilling chase saw Essex start the first post-war season with a two-wicket victory over Somerset at Taunton. They had been set 383 and began the final day on 59 for 3. There seemed little prospect of victory when half the side had been dismissed for 109, but captain Tom Pearce found support from the lower order. He put on 57 for the sixth wicket with Robert Paterson and 81 for the seventh wicket with Ernest Tedder. Then a stand of 93 with Ray Smith turned the match decisively in Essex's favour. Smith was eighth out with 43 needed, but Pearce and Tom Wade knocked off the runs, with Pearce remaining unbeaten at the finish on 166.

FRIDAY 14th MAY 2010

Police arrested Essex bowlers Danish Kaneria and Mervyn Westfield as part of an investigation into the county's NatWest Pro40 match against Durham the previous September. In that match — which Essex won by seven wickets — Westfield had bowled seven overs for 60 and conceded two no-balls and four wides, while Kaneria had taken 2 for 58 from eight overs with two wides. The enquiry was one of several at the time into allegations that players had collaborated in illegal betting schemes by bowling wides or no-balls to order. Kaneria was later released without charge, but Westfield eventually admitted a charge of corruption. Westfield did not play for Essex again, and Kaneria's contract was not renewed at the end of the season.

SATURDAY 15th MAY 1948

Australia scored 721 all out from 129 overs — a world record for the most runs compiled in a single day — on the first day of their tour match against Essex at Southend. Four Australian batsmen — Brown, Bradman, Loxton, and Saggers — scored centuries as the tourists maintained a scoring rate of just over five and a half runs per over through each of the three sessions. Peter Smith, who ended with 4 for 193 from 38 overs, took three quick wickets at the end of the day to finish off the innings. This was the only time during the entire summer that the Australian side was dismissed inside a day.

SUNDAY 15th MAY 1966

Essex broke new ground by being the first county to include Sunday play in a Championship match. A crowd of around 6,000 turned up at Ilford to watch the second day against Somerset, although Essex only managed to capture two wickets while 238 runs were scored. The financial success of the venture prompted the Essex committee to include Sunday play in matches in the following season. The idea of playing championship cricket on a Sunday was put on hold with the inception of the John Player League in 1969, but has since become commonplace.

FRIDAY 15th MAY 1998

Danny Law took a hat-trick on the third day of Essex's match against Durham at Chester-le-Street. He dismissed Michael Foster, Nicky Phillips, and Melvyn Betts to reduce the home side to 177 for 8 in their second innings. However, Durham already led by 268, and the last two wickets extended this lead to 338. Essex were in trouble at 196 for 6 at the close, and would lose the following day.

WEDNESDAY 16th MAY 1956

Doug Insole and Trevor Bailey both scored centuries on the first day of Essex's match against Kent at Dartford. The pair added 166 for the fourth wicket with Insole hitting 122 and Bailey 108, as the county reached a total of 361. This proved to be a more than sufficient total as Kent were bowled out twice on the following day and Essex won by nine wickets.

THURSDAY 16th MAY 1957

A year to the day after performing the feat at Dartford, Doug Insole and Trevor Bailey again both scored centuries on the same day — this time against Glamorgan at Ilford. On this occasion, Insole had a significant head start, resuming overnight on 62 and scoring most of his 106 runs in a third-wicket partnership of 154 with Gordon Barker. This established a lead which Bailey's unbeaten 102 extended to 250, and Essex declared on 396 for 7. The bowlers were unable to force a victory on the final day, however, and the match was drawn.

THURSDAY 16th MAY 1985

John Lever produced 5 for 13 from his 11 overs to wreck the Middlesex innings and set up a win for Essex in a Benson and Hedges Cup group match at Lord's. Lever dismissed five of Middlesex's top six to reduce the home side to 27 for 6. They were eventually all out for 73, and Essex won, not without a few alarms, by four wickets.

MONDAY 17th MAY 1948

The county suffered its largest margin of defeat — an innings and 451 runs — against Australia at Southend. The match resumed after Australia's record-setting first innings of 721 on the Saturday, and Essex, handicapped by the absence of Trevor Bailey, who had broken a finger in the field, were bowled out before lunch for 83. They were soon 46 for 6 in their second innings, but Tom Pearce (71) and Peter Smith (54) helped them reach 187. Nevertheless, the county was bowled out twice inside a day to mark the end of a most one-sided contest.

TUESDAY 18th MAY 1915

John Pawle was born in Widford, Hertfordshire. He played six first-class matches for Essex between 1935 and 1938, scoring 194 runs at 17.63. He had more success when playing for Cambridge University, hitting three centuries in 20 matches. Pawle served in World War Two and afterwards worked as a stockbroker. In later life he dedicated himself to painting and had his work exhibited in numerous galleries. He died in 2010 at the age of 94.

THURSDAY 19th MAY 1859

Hugh Owen was born in Bath. He first played for Essex in 1880 and continued until 1902, captaining the side from 1895 until his retirement. He was the first player to make a century for the club against another county side, and the first to make a century for Essex in a first-class match. David Lemmon and Mike Marshall describe him in their history of the club as "genial, ever smiling and popular", and credit him with instilling the sense of fun that would become a hallmark of Essex cricket.

SATURDAY 19th MAY 1973

Graham Gooch made his debut aged 19 in a Benson and Hedges Cup group match against Surrey at Chelmsford. He batted at number eight, and started his innings just before play was suspended with Essex needing 49 to win from 8.2 overs. When play resumed on the Monday he was bowled by Intikhab Alam for two as Essex fell 16 short. Things would get much better for him over the next 25 years.

THURSDAY 19th MAY 2011

Graham Napier equalled the record for the number of sixes in a first-class innings when hitting 196 from just 130 balls against Surrey. Napier's innings had begun the previous day, when he finished unbeaten on 25 with the Essex total on 318 for 6. Looking for quick runs, Napier took advantage of the short boundaries at Croydon's Whitgift School, clearing the ropes 16 times. He also struck 19 fours. Chris Wright had a first-hand view of the carnage as the pair put on 190 for the ninth wicket in 22.2 overs, with Wright's share just 34. The pair were then both out within four balls, leaving Essex's final total at 548. Surrey made a strong showing in reply, however, and ended the day on 277 for 4 as the match headed towards a draw.

SATURDAY 20th MAY 1899

Essex beat Sussex by one wicket in a tense finish at Ilford. Sussex had scored 142 in their first innings, with Walter Mead taking 7 for 34. Essex's reply of 191 owed much to Charlie McGahey's unbeaten 75. Sussex then scored 180, Mead taking a further three wickets, to leave Essex needing a modest 132 to win. They began the last day on 15 for 1 and lost captain Hugh Owen without adding a run. McGahey made only three this time, but 48 from Johnny Turner saw the county close in, although the scoring rate crept along at less than two runs per over and wickets fell at regular intervals. Four runs were still required when the last pair of Frederick Bull and Sailor Young came together, but they kept their nerve to take Essex over the finishing line.

SATURDAY 20th MAY 1944

Keith Fletcher was born in Worcester. Between 1962 and 1988 he played in 574 first-class matches for the county — more than any other player — scoring 29,434 runs at an average of 36.88. He struck 45 centuries, with a top score of 228 not out against Sussex at Hastings in 1968. His total of runs for the county is second only to that of Graham Gooch, and his 519 catches constitute the most by a non-wicketkeeper. Fletcher captained Essex from 1974 to 1985 and led the club to its first trophies, the Benson and Hedges Cup and the County Championship in 1979. His tenure represents a golden age of Essex cricket, with more championship successes following in 1983 and 1984, as well as four further one-day trophies. He played in 59 Tests for England, including seven as captain, scoring seven centuries and averaging 39.90. He later coached the county side, and from 1993 to 1995 was the England team manager.

TUESDAY 20th MAY 1947

Essex's match against Northamptonshire at Ilford ended in a tie after the county had been set 240 to win on the last day. A fourth-wicket partnership of 103 between Frank Vigar (60) and Len Clark (64) put Essex into a strong position at 166 for 3, but the lower order struggled against the spin of Broderick and Clarke. Eleven were still needed when the last man, Tom Wade, came in to join Tom Pearce. The pair had managed only ten when Wade was bowled. The last wicket was taken by Bertie Clarke, who would later play for Essex.

THURSDAY 21st MAY 1970

Jonathan Lewis was born in Isleworth, Middlesex. He played 58 first-class matches for Essex between 1990 and 1996, scoring 2,959 runs at an average of 34.01, including four centuries — one of which was on his debut. His highest score for the county was 136 not out against Nottinghamshire at Trent Bridge in 1993, made in an unbroken stand of 242 for the second wicket with John Stephenson. Lewis joined Durham in 1997 — this time scoring a double-century on his debut — and played a further ten seasons, four as captain, before retiring in 2006.

FRIDAY 21st MAY 2010

Essex beat Holland by one run in their Clydesdale Bank 40 group match at Amstelveen. The Dutch restricted Essex to 218 for 8, Matt Walker top-scoring with 71. This target looked vulnerable as Eric Szwarczynski and Baz Zuiderent added 103 for the fourth wicket. When the last over started only six were needed with five wickets left, but Craig Wright allowed just three runs from his first five balls. From the last ball Mudassar Bukhari was run out attempting a second run that would have tied the match.

SATURDAY 22nd MAY 1920

Roy Ralph was born in East Ham. He played 174 first-class matches for the county between 1953 and 1961, taking 460 wickets with his medium-pace swing bowling at an average of 24.02 and scoring 3,763 runs at 16.87. His best bowling performance came in 1956 against Gloucestershire at Ilford when he took 7 for 42 as Essex won by an innings.

SATURDAY 22nd MAY 2004

Essex reached their second highest first-class total, 708 for 9 against Leicestershire (who had also suffered the highest total 14 years earlier). They went out to bat facing a total of 520. However, by the start of the final day they had passed Leicestershire's score, thanks to centuries from Alastair Cook (his maiden first-class hundred), Will Jefferson, and James Foster, while Aftab Habib hit 97. They batted on for 6.4 overs, adding 43 runs, 33 of which were scored by Foster, who took his score to 212 (a new career best) before being caught at the wicket. Leicestershire then batted out the rest of the day to escape with a draw.

TUESDAY 23rd MAY 1905

Charlie McGahey hit a career-best score of 277 to rescue his side and set up a victory against Derbyshire at Leyton. Replying to Derbyshire's 367, Essex found themselves 65 for 5, but McGahey put on 167 with Johnny Turner and then found good support from the lower order before being ninth out. They eventually declared on 507 and bowled Derbyshire out on the last day to win by an innings.

MONDAY 24th MAY 2004

Nasser Hussain ended his Test career in style with a century against New Zealand at Lord's. He had relinquished the captaincy the previous year but retained his place in the side. On the last day of the first Test England chased 282 and were 35 for 2 when Hussain came in. He added 108 for the third wicket with debutant Andrew Strauss and then 139 with Graham Thorpe as England won by seven wickets. He brought up his century from the penultimate ball of the match and finished not out on 103. Three days after this innings he announced his retirement from all forms of cricket and began a career as a television commentator.

WEDNESDAY 25th MAY 1921

Essex captain Johnny Douglas produced a brilliant all-round performance against Derbyshire at Leyton. Derbyshire batted first and Douglas bowled unchanged, except for one over, taking 9 for 47 from 26.2 overs. Seven of the opposition were dismissed without the help of his fielders. However, Derbyshire's total of 114 seemed like it might still be competitive when Essex were reduced to 19 for 4. Douglas then took charge with the bat, ending the day on 62 not out and leading a recovery to 138 for 7. There was still a lot of work to do, and Douglas was just the man to do it over the next two days as he took his personal score to a small matter of 210.

TUESDAY 25th MAY 1982

Graham Gooch hit 198 not out against Sussex in the Benson and Hedges Cup group match at Hove. Gooch's innings was the highest score by any player in the 31-year history of the competition, containing five sixes and 22 fours, and came against a side fielding the vaunted pace attack of Imran Khan and Garth le Roux. Keith Fletcher also scored a century and he and Gooch put on an unbeaten stand of 268 for the third wicket as Essex finished on 327 for 2 from their 55 overs. Sussex were then bowled out for 213 — Gooch chipping in with three wickets — to leave Essex winners by 114 runs, but Sussex qualified from the group.

SATURDAY 26th MAY 1900

Essex beat Surrey by five runs at The Oval. The county led by 15 on first innings thanks to 95 from Percy Perrin. However, they were then bowled out for 68 in 17.4 overs, leaving Surrey 84 to win. Walter Mead and Charles Kortright bowled unchanged and had Surrey 34 for 7 before William Brockwell scored 28 not out to take Surrey to the brink of victory at 78 for 8. However, Mead bowled Lees and Wood with consecutive deliveries to win it for Essex.

TUESDAY 26th MAY 1959

Essex won a close encounter with Northamptonshire at Ilford by two runs. They led by 143 on first innings, but were skittled out for 127 on the last morning, leaving Northamptonshire to chase 271 in four hours. They had reached 268 for 7 when Ken Preston began the last over, but lost their last three wickets in four balls without adding a run.

THURSDAY 26th MAY 1977

Ray East took 8 for 30 as Essex bowled out Nottinghamshire for 81 on their way to a two-day victory at Ilford. East came on in the third over of Nottinghamshire's second innings and exploited the turning conditions brilliantly in a 21-over spell, helped by four close-to-the-wicket catches by Keith Fletcher. Essex were left to score 97 to win and won by six wickets, Ken McEwan top-scoring with 32.

FRIDAY 27th MAY 1921

Johnny Douglas and Steriker Hare took their ninth-wicket partnership against Derbyshire to 251 — a county record. The pair had added 194 on the previous, rain-interrupted day as Essex took control of the match. On the final day, Douglas reached 210 with 28 fours, the only double-century of his career, while debutant Hare was eventually out just two runs short of a century. Derbyshire faced a first-innings deficit of 282 and were all out for 208. Douglas, who had rested himself at the start of the Derbyshire innings after his exertions with the bat, came on to take the second new ball and wrapped up the match by taking two wickets for no runs.

TUESDAY 27th MAY 1947

Essex beat Worcestershire by one wicket at New Road with two balls to spare. The county had trailed by 111 on first innings despite an unbeaten 137 from skipper Tom Pearce. Ray Smith then took six wickets in Worcestershire's second innings to restrict the target to 284. Again Pearce took the leading role, but he was seventh out for 96 with 73 still needed. However, Smith hit 57 and then Tom Wade struck two fours in the last available over to snatch a dramatic victory.

MONDAY 28th MAY 1917

Bill Morris was born in Kingston, Jamaica. He played 48 first-class matches for the county between 1946 and 1950, scoring 1,219 runs at 17.92 and taking 43 wickets with his leg-breaks at an average of 45.93. He later played a major role in developing future Essex players (including Graham Gooch and John Lever) as a coach in the indoor cricket school at Ilford.

TUESDAY 28th MAY 1957

Essex beat Hampshire by 46 runs at Romford. The match was a personal triumph for Trevor Bailey who top-scored in both Essex innings with 59 and 71 not out and took 6 for 32 when Hampshire batted. However, only one other Essex player had managed to pass 20 in the match, and Hampshire's final target was a very modest 163. Bailey now took 8 for 49 as Essex bowled them out for 116. Bailey's match figures of 14 for 81 were the best of his career.

THURSDAY 29th MAY 1919

Thomas "Dickie" Dodds was born in Bedford. An opening batsman, he played 380 first-class matches for Essex between 1946 and 1959, scoring 18,565 runs at an average of 28.73. He scored 17 centuries and passed 1,000 runs in 13 consecutive seasons. He also took 36 wickets at an average of 31.27. Dodds was noted for his aggressive stroke-play, which was never more evident than in a match against Sussex in 1953 when he hit the first ball of the Essex innings for six. He died in Cambridge in 2001 at the age of 82.

SUNDAY 29th MAY 1977

Essex beat Lancashire by one wicket in a John Player League match at Ilford. Lancashire batted first and scored 164 for 7 from their 40 overs. Essex appeared on course for a comfortable win as Graham Gooch and Stuart Turner added 48 for the first wicket, but Lancashire's slower bowlers wrested back the initiative, David Hughes taking 4 for 19. Seven were needed from the last over with the last pair, John Lever and David Acfield, together. The third ball went for four byes, and Essex scrambled home with a ball to spare.

SATURDAY 29th MAY 2004

Will Jefferson and Andy Flower added 248 for the first wicket against Nottinghamshire in the third round of the Cheltenham and Gloucester Trophy at Trent Bridge. Jefferson hit 126 from 125 balls with 17 fours, while Flower's 106 was made from 127 balls with ten fours. Essex built on this platform to reach 309 for 4. Graham Napier then dismissed Kevin Pietersen and David Hussey for first-ball ducks as Nottinghamshire were all out for 125 in 21.2 overs, leaving Essex winners by 184 runs.

WEDNESDAY 30th MAY 1962

A young player called Geoff Hurst made his debut for Essex against Lancashire at Liverpool, although he failed to score a run in either innings. It would be his only appearance for Essex, as professional football took priority: he scored over 200 goals for West Ham United, Stoke City, and West Bromwich Albion and memorably scored a hat-trick for England in the World Cup Final in 1966. He was knighted in 1998.

SUNDAY 30th MAY 1971

Keith Boyce produced the best one-day bowling figures in the county's history, taking 8 for 26 against Lancashire at Old Trafford. The match was interrupted by rain and Lancashire faced a revised target of 97 from 17 overs. Boyce ripped through the batting, bowling four of his victims, to leave them ten runs short. It was the first time that any player had taken eight wickets in a one-day match, and the feat was not repeated until 1987.

MONDAY 30th MAY 1983

Norbert Phillip and Neil Foster sensationally bowled out Surrey for 14 — easily the lowest total ever scored against Essex. The first day of the match at Chelmsford had been lost to rain, and Essex were bowled out for 287 an hour before the end of day two, with Keith Fletcher scoring 110. Surrey then went in to bat and suffered a collective calamity: only four batsmen managed to score as Phillip took 6 for 4 and Foster 4 for 10. At one stage five wickets fell without a run being added, and the whole innings was completed in just 14.3 overs. However, a combination of rain and more resolute Surrey batting the following day deprived Essex of a victory.

THURSDAY 31st MAY 1934

Kent declared their first innings closed on 803 for 4 — the highest total ever conceded by Essex in a first-class match. The Kent score featured three huge individual scores, with Bill Ashdown making 332, Frank Woolley 172, and Les Ames 202 not out. Eight different bowlers were tried by Essex, with Peter Smith suffering the worst with figures of 0 for 208 from 36 overs. Essex put up some resistance when they finally got to bat and finished the day on 366 for 7, with a century from Dudley Pope and Jack O'Connor on 80 not out. However, they would capitulate on the next day on a deteriorating Brentwood pitch and lost the game by an innings and 192 runs.

ESSEX CCC
On This Day

JUNE

FRIDAY 1st JUNE 1951

Ray Smith hit the fastest hundred of the season during a daring run-chase in Essex's match against South Africa at Ilford. South Africa declared on the final day setting Essex an improbable 280 in two and a half hours. They perhaps did not reckon on Smith hitting a whirlwind 147, and adding 182 for the second wicket with Dick Horsfall in less than an hour and a half. Even so, Essex could only manage 255 for 5 before time ran out, and the match was drawn.

SATURDAY 2nd JUNE 1906

Walter Mead took 7 for 13 as Essex beat Derbyshire by 209 runs at Leyton. Mead and Claude Buckenham bowled unchanged through the second innings and dismissed the visitors for 53 in just 16.1 overs. Mead had not played for Essex in the previous two seasons owing to a financial dispute, and this was his first five-wicket haul since returning to the club.

WEDNESDAY 2nd JUNE 1965

Mark Waugh was born in Sydney. One of Australia's finest batsmen, he played 128 Tests and scored over 8,000 runs. He joined Essex on the recommendation of Allan Border — his immediate predecessor as the county's overseas player — and played 82 first-class matches for the club between 1988 and 2002. He scored 6,690 runs at 59.73, with 22 centuries and a highest score of 219 not out against Lancashire in 1992, when he shared in an unbroken third-wicket partnership of 347 with Nasser Hussain. He also took 65 wickets at 42.07 and was a brilliant slip fielder, taking 101 catches in his Essex career.

MONDAY 2nd JUNE 1975

Play in the match between Essex and Kent at Colchester was delayed by heavy snowfall. Graham Gooch remembers the effect that the two inches of snow had on the uncovered pitch: "The next day I was out caught Mike Denness bowled Norman Graham from a ball which went up my nose!" However, the tricky conditions ultimately worked to Essex's advantage as Stuart Turner and Ray East dismissed Kent to secure a 33-run victory.

MONDAY 3rd JUNE 1895

Harry Pickett returned the best figures by an Essex bowler, taking 10 for 32 as Leicestershire were bowled out for 111 on the first day at Leyton. The contemporary report in *Cricket* described the pitch as "fast and somewhat fiery" but paid tribute to the bowler for maintaining a "splendid length". Pickett bowled unchanged for 27 five-ball overs while Walter Mead and Charles Kortright went wicketless at the other end. However, his heroics went unrewarded as Essex were bowled out for 103 and 123 and lost the match by 75 runs.

SATURDAY 3rd JUNE 1950

Essex's match against Warwickshire at Ilford was the first involving the county to be televised. The BBC paid a fee of £75 to cover the proceedings. Ray Smith took five wickets as Warwickshire were dismissed for 335, and Doug Insole scored a century when Essex batted, but there was little else to excite the viewers in a drawn game.

WEDNESDAY 4th JUNE 2008

Ravi Bopara became the first Essex player to make a double-century in a limited-overs match, hitting 201 not out against Leicestershire in the quarter-final of the Friends Provident Trophy. Bopara did not even have the advantage of batting through the entire 50 overs of the innings but came in at number four with the score at 34 for 2. He made his runs from 138 balls with ten sixes and 18 fours, helping Essex to a total of 350 for 5. He then took two wickets as Leicestershire were all out for 232, leaving Essex winners by 118 runs.

MONDAY 5th JUNE 1922

Essex enjoyed one of their most emphatic victories, beating Worcestershire by an innings and 297 runs at Leyton. George Louden and Johnny Douglas had bowled the visitors out for 49 on the first morning, and Joseph Dixon and John Freeman scored centuries as Essex racked up 521 at nearly five an over. Worcestershire faced a huge deficit and were bowled out in their second innings for 175. Leg-spinner Philip Morris took 7 for 43 as Essex completed the win inside two days.

MONDAY 5th JUNE 1978

Graham Gooch and Ken McEwan added 321 — then an Essex record — for the second wicket against Northamptonshire at Ilford. The pair both fell with the score on 339, Gooch for 129 and McEwan a superb 186, including a six and 26 fours. Essex advanced to 457 for 5 before declaring and went on to win by an innings.

SATURDAY 6th JUNE 1891

Essex pulled off a sensational victory over Leicestershire at Leyton thanks to the bowling of Walter Mead. Set just 115 to win, Leicestershire were skittled out for 67, with Mead taking an astonishing 9 for 23. Moreover, eight of his victims were bowled. After the match a collection was held for him — as was customary at that time when a professional player had made an outstanding contribution — and raised the sum of five pounds and ten shillings.

SATURDAY 6th JUNE 1931

Gordon Barker was born in the Bramley district of Leeds. He played 444 first-class matches for Essex between 1954 and 1971, forming regular opening partnerships with first Dickie Dodds and then Geoff Smith. He scored 21,895 runs — an aggregate that places him sixth on the all-time list of run-scorers for the county — at an average of 29.15. Among his 30 centuries was a highest score of 181 not out against Kent at Colchester in 1961. Barker also played professional football as a winger for Southend United, scoring nine goals in 57 appearances. He died at Chelmsford in 2006 at the age of 74.

SUNDAY 6th JUNE 1971

Essex bowled Northamptonshire out for 45 in a John Player League match at Ilford. It was the second-lowest total ever made against the county in the competition. Keith Boyce made the early inroads with 4 for 10 in eight overs, while David Acfield took 3 for 13 in eight overs as Northamptonshire took 28.1 overs to limp to their sorry total. Brian Crump, who top-scored with 18, was the only batsman to reach double figures. Bruce Francis and Tonker Taylor then took Essex to a ten-wicket victory in only 12.2 overs.

FRIDAY 6th JUNE 1997

Nasser Hussain hit his highest Test score of 207 on the second day of the first Test between England and Australia at Edgbaston. England had gone in as clear underdogs and surprised everyone by bowling Australia out for 118 on the first day. Hussain was joined by Graham Thorpe with England's reply on 50 for 3 and they added 288 to put England into a commanding position. Hussain batted for over seven hours and struck 38 fours before being caught behind off the bowling of Shane Warne. England went on to win the match by nine wickets and take a short-lived series lead.

THURSDAY 7th JUNE 1900

Herbert Williams was born in Hendon, Middlesex. He was a wicketkeeper who played ten first-class matches for the county in 1919 and 1920, scoring 67 runs at 6.70 with 18 catches and seven stumpings. Williams later moved to Brazil and represented that country in several matches against Argentina towards the end of the 1920s. He died in London in 1974.

MONDAY 8th JUNE 1936

Stan Nichols achieved his career-best bowling figures 9 for 32 against Nottinghamshire at Trent Bridge. He was robbed of the chance to capture all ten when Arthur Staples was run out. Nevertheless, his effort saw Nottinghamshire dismissed for 77 and gave Essex a first-innings lead of 94. As was the case with many fine individual performances by Essex players down the years, however, Nichols was to end up on the losing side. The Nottinghamshire openers put on an unbeaten stand of 201 in the second innings and Essex lost by ten wickets.

FRIDAY 8th JUNE 1962

Essex beat Kent by one wicket at Romford. Essex had taken a large first-innings lead thanks to a century from Michael Bear, but were then held up by centuries from Peter Richardson and Bob Wilson. Chasing 152 to win on the last afternoon, Essex lost wickets regularly and 16 were still needed when the last man Paddy Phelan joined Trevor Bailey. Phelan made 16 on his own, hitting the winning runs with two balls to spare.

TUESDAY 9th JUNE 1908

Essex beat Gloucestershire by the enormous margin of an innings and 275 runs at Leyton. Gloucestershire had been bowled out for 94 by Johnny Douglas and Claude Buckenham on the previous day, and Charlie McGahey and Frank Gillingham had batted Essex into a comfortable lead by the close. On the second day Gillingham added a century before lunch as the fourth-wicket partnership was extended to 181. Gillingham eventually reached 194, with 22 fours, and McGahey 126, as Essex totalled 436. Douglas and Buckenham routed Gloucestershire — who were without two injured batsmen — for 67 in their second innings to bring the contest to a hasty conclusion. Douglas finished with 6 for 29 and match figures of 12 for 74.

WEDNESDAY 9th JUNE 1920

Percy Toone took a remarkable hat-trick against Kent at Leyton. The Kent opening pair of Wally Hardinge and George Collins put on 66 against Douglas, Dixon, Russell, and Reeves before Toone became the fifth bowler introduced into the attack. In a sensational start he had Collins caught by Jack Russell off his first ball and then dismissed James Seymour in identical fashion with his second. The great Frank Woolley now came out and was bowled first ball to complete Toone's hat-trick. The bowler took only one more wicket in the innings, finishing with 4 for 74 as Kent recovered to 326, and the match was drawn. Toone also managed his highest first-class score of 24 in the same game.

SUNDAY 9th JUNE 1991

Graham Gooch carried his bat for 154 in the first Test match between England and the West Indies at Headingley. He batted for seven and a half hours and hit 18 fours while no other batsman scored more than 27. Gooch's Essex team-mate Derek Pringle supported him in a crucial stand of 98 for the seventh wicket. England were all out for 252, which was the highest score of the match and set up a 115-run victory. The PricewaterhouseCoopers rating system, which takes into account the quality of the opposition bowling and the relative difficulty of scoring runs in the match, ranks this as the best Test innings by any player since World War Two.

TUESDAY 9th JUNE 1998

Essex reached their second consecutive Lord's final by beating Yorkshire in the semi-final of the Benson and Hedges Cup at Headingley. They recovered from losing Darren Robinson to the first ball of the match and scored 258 for 7 from their 50 overs, with Nasser Hussain top-scoring on 78. Yorkshire never seriously threatened to challenge this score and fell 95 runs short, with Paul Grayson taking 3 for 32 against his former county.

MONDAY 10th JUNE 1878

Arthur Jervois "Johnny" Turner was born in Mussoorie (now Musuri) in India. He played 68 first-class matches for Essex between 1897 and 1910, scoring 3,760 runs at an average of 35.86 with 11 centuries. However, his cricket career took second place to a career as a soldier. He served with the Royal Artillery in the Boer War (where he was wounded at Ladysmith) and the First World War, reaching the rank of brigadier and receiving the Distinguished Service Order and the Croix de Guerre. Turner died in Graffham, Sussex, in 1952 at the age of 74.

FRIDAY 10th JUNE 1904

Claude Buckenham returned career-best figures as Essex inflicted a crushing victory on Sussex at Leyton. Essex scored 425 in their first innings, with Percy Perrin hitting 190. Buckenham then bowled unchanged for 18.2 overs and took 8 for 33 as Sussex could muster only 87. The follow-on was enforced, and Bill Reeves and Bert Tremlin now shared the wickets as the visitors were dismissed for 134 to leave Essex winners by an innings and 204 runs.

TUESDAY 10th JUNE 1952

Bill Greensmith completed an exceptional all-round match by bowling out Leicestershire on the last day at Hinckley. On the Saturday he had come in at number ten and hit 79 out of a ninth-wicket partnership of 139 with Frank Vigar. That contribution helped Essex establish a first-innings lead of 128, and Leicestershire were eventually set a target of 283 on a turning pitch. Greensmith took 6 for 44, at one stage taking five wickets without conceding a run, as Essex won by 107 runs.

TUESDAY 11th JUNE 1974

Essex's match with Sussex at Hove ended in a tie. Time had been lost at the start, and two declarations were needed on the last day, with Essex set 219 to win. They struggled against the spin of Waller and Joshi, and were 122 for 6 when a young batsman called Graham Gooch came out at number eight in only his third first-class match. He added 70 with Stuart Turner to take Essex within sight of victory before fast bowler John Snow returned to take two wickets (including Gooch for 44). Essex lost their last three wickets for five runs and had to settle for a share of the spoils.

SATURDAY 12th JUNE 1948

West Indian all-rounder Norbert Phillip was born in Bioche, on the island of Dominica. He played 144 first-class matches for Essex between 1978 and 1985, taking 423 wickets at an average of 25.14 while also scoring 3,784 runs at 21.13. His best bowling figures were the remarkable six wickets for four runs when he and Neil Foster dismissed Surrey for 14 at Chelmsford in 1983, while his only century was a match-winning 134 against Gloucestershire in 1978. Phillip also featured prominently in a number of one-day trophy successes during his time at the club. He played nine Tests for the West Indies during the period when many established stars were playing World Series Cricket, scoring 297 runs at 29.70 and taking 28 wickets at 37.17.

FRIDAY 12th JUNE 1964

Off-spinner Peter Such was born in Helensburgh, Scotland. He grew up in the East Midlands and played for both Nottinghamshire and Leicestershire before joining Essex in 1990. He played 189 first-class matches for the county before his retirement in 2001, taking 573 wickets at an average of 29.68. He formed a successful spin partnership with John Childs, and made a significant contribution to Essex's title wins in 1991 and 1992, although his best performance of 8 for 93 came against Hampshire in 1995. His batting was much maligned, and yet he hit two 50s and featured in some crucial partnerships for the county. He also played in 11 Tests for England between 1993 and 1999, taking 37 wickets at 33.56.

TUESDAY 12th JUNE 1984

Essex beat Warwickshire by 35 runs at Ilford despite suffering a first-innings deficit of 220 and being made to follow on. Essex managed to get back into the game in their second innings thanks to scores of 92 from Chris Gladwin and 97 from Ken McEwan, but they could only set their opponents a target of 155 to win. John Lever took two early wickets to give Essex hope, and David Acfield then dismissed Paul Smith and Dennis Amiss after the pair had put on 52. Two more wickets from Lever left Warwickshire in deep trouble at 68 for 6. They then progressed to 100 for 6 before Derek Pringle came back to take the last four wickets. This unlikely victory was to prove crucial at the end of the season as Essex pipped Nottinghamshire to the title.

MONDAY 13th JUNE 1921

John Freeman reached 286 against Northamptonshire — the second-highest individual score by an Essex player in first-class matches. He resumed on 218 and batted for seven hours in all, hitting 38 fours and one six, and sharing in partnerships of 189 for the second wicket with Jack Russell, 152 for the third wicket with Percy Perrin, and 130 for the fourth wicket with George Carter. Essex eventually declared on 604 for 7. Freeman was still sufficiently fresh after his marathon innings to take two stumpings in his role as wicketkeeper, but, although Northamptonshire were made to follow on, the match was drawn.

TUESDAY 13th JUNE 1978

Essex beat Gloucestershire by two wickets in a pulsating finish. Set 313 to win, they lost Mike Denness, Graham Gooch, Ken McEwan, and Keith Fletcher with only 120 on the board, leaving victory a distant prospect. However, Norbert Phillip now came in and struck seven sixes in a blazing 134 — his only first-class century — and was particularly severe on John Childs. He found support from Brian Hardie, with whom he added 106 for the fifth wicket, and Ray East. Phillip's onslaught was ended in the last over by Mike Procter, but Essex were now just one run in arrears. John Lever came in and scored the winning runs off the last ball.

SUNDAY 13th JUNE 1982

Norbert Phillip took 6 for 13 in 6.2 overs in Essex's John Player League match against Lancashire at Old Trafford. The figures are made more remarkable because no other bowler found conditions to their liking: Essex made 269 for 3 from their 40 overs, Graham Gooch leading the way with 122. Phillip then reduced Lancashire to 18 for 3, but when he was withdrawn from the attack Frank Hayes engineered a recovery with 87. However, Phillip returned to take three more wickets (including that of Hayes), and Essex won by 82 runs.

MONDAY 13th JUNE 1994

Essex successfully chased 405 to beat Worcestershire at New Road. Worcestershire had seemed in control of the match from the start and declared shortly before the close on the third day. Essex had lost three wickets for 133 when Graham Gooch was joined by Ronnie Irani. The pair added 245 for the fourth wicket, with Gooch scoring 205 and Irani 119. Both batsmen fell within sight of victory, but Nadeem Shahid saw Essex home. It was only the third time in the club's history that Essex had scored more than 400 in the fourth innings of a match.

SUNDAY 13th JUNE 2010

Ryan ten Doeschate became the fourth player to score a century for Essex in a Twenty20 match, hitting 102 against Middlesex at Lord's. The runs came in just 54 balls with five fours and seven sixes, but were still not enough to bring Essex a win. Middlesex had batted first and scored 200 for 6 from their 20 overs — despite no batsman passing 50. Essex lost two early wickets and were always behind the required rate. When ten Doeschate fell in the penultimate over there were still 23 required, and the county eventually lost by five runs.

WEDNESDAY 14th JUNE 1905

Johns Inns died in his home village of Writtle at the age of only 29. He played ten first-class matches for the county between 1898 and 1904, scoring 73 runs at 6.63 and occasionally filling in as an emergency wicketkeeper.

SATURDAY 15th JUNE 1895

Essex recorded their first victory in the County Championship, beating Somerset by two wickets at Leyton. Somerset had batted first and made 191, Harry Pickett and Walter Mead taking the last four wickets for one run. Essex made 181 in reply, Frederick Fane top-scoring on his debut with 36. Mead then took his second five-wicket haul of the match as Somerset were bowled out for 177, leaving Essex to chase 188. They began the last day on 101 for 4, and made steady progress to 165 for 5, whereupon three wickets fell without a run being scored. However, there were no further alarms as Charles Kortright and Frederick Bull added the remaining runs. The win came in the county's fifth match of its inaugural campaign and was the first of five victories in the championship that season.

THURSDAY 15th JUNE 1899

Walter Mead became the first Essex player to win a Test cap, appearing for England in the second match of the Ashes series at Lord's. He was given plenty of opportunity, bowling 51 overs in Australia's first innings and taking 1 for 91. Australia won by ten wickets — the only decisive result of the series — and Mead, who had proved economical but not penetrating, was not selected again. Ironically, his place went to another Essex player, Sailor Young.

THURSDAY 15th JUNE 1995

Mark Ilott took the remarkable figures of 9 for 19 against Northamptonshire at Luton. Even more remarkably, Essex contrived to lose the match. They batted first in cloudy conditions and were dismissed for 127, with Robert Rollins scoring 52 not out. Ilott now came to the fore, troubling all of the Northamptonshire batsmen with his swing bowling. Two of his victims were bowled and six were out leg-before-wicket, including three — Snape, Kumble, and Mallender — in consecutive deliveries to complete an unusual hat-trick. The last five wickets fell without a run scored, and Northamptonshire were dismissed for 46. However, Essex were bowled out again before the close, this time for 107. On the second day conditions were slightly easier. Ilott claimed a further five victims, but Northamptonshire made 192 for 8 to win by two wickets.

TUESDAY 16th JUNE 1891

Charles Kortright set a new record for the highest individual score for the fledgling county, 158 in under two hours against Hampshire at Southampton. He came in at number eight and put on 244 with Harry Pickett, who scored 114. The partnership helped Essex reach 424 and they won by an innings. Kortright became much better known as a bowler over the next 15 years, and he never bettered this score.

SATURDAY 16th JUNE 1906

Essex beat the West Indies by 111 runs at Leyton. They trailed by 153 after the first innings, but Percy Perrin hit a century then Claude Buckenham and Walter Mead added 95 for the last wicket to set the tourists 243 to win. Mead took two early wickets and Buckenham captured 4 for 41 as Essex bowled out the visitors for 131.

THURSDAY 16th JUNE 1932

The Essex bowling was destroyed at Leyton by the Yorkshire opening pair of Herbert Sutcliffe and Percy Holmes. Yorkshire had batted all through the first day, scoring 423 without loss. On the second day the first-wicket partnership continued until the total passed the existing record of 554, at which point Sutcliffe was bowled by Laurie Eastman for 313. Yorkshire promptly declared at 555 for 1, Holmes's share of the stand being 224. There was a moment of confusion as the scorers could not agree on the total, but Essex's stand-in captain Charlie Bray magnanimously agreed a run should be found to ensure that the record stood. The extra run would make no difference to the result: Hedley Verity took ten wickets as the demoralised Essex side was bowled out for 78 and 164 to lose by an innings.

FRIDAY 17th JUNE 1966

Essex beat Kent by four runs in a low-scoring match at Dartford. Derek Underwood took 6 for 20 in Essex's second innings as they were bowled out for 112, leaving Kent to score a mere 87 to win. They were all out for 82 with Brian Edmeades taking 4 for 29 and Trevor Bailey 3 for 25.

FRIDAY 18th JUNE 1926

Essex's match against Somerset at Chelmsford ended controversially. Essex needed 138 to win on the last day, but rain prevented any play until mid-afternoon. The scores were level when Laurie Eastman was ninth out from the last ball of the 58th over, and Gerald Ridley sprinted to the wicket. However, the umpires ruled that there was no time to start another over. This left the match drawn, Somerset taking three points to Essex's one by virtue of leading on first innings. After an appeal the match was officially deemed a tie and both sides received 2.5 points.

SUNDAY 19th JUNE 1932

Brian "Tonker" Taylor was born in West Ham. He played 539 first-class matches for Essex as a wicketkeeper-batsman between 1949 and 1973, including a run of 301 consecutive appearances between 1961 and 1972. He scored 18,239 runs at 21.92, including nine centuries, and passed 1,000 runs in a season eight times. Taylor holds the record for the most dismissals by an Essex wicketkeeper with 1,205 (1,014 catches and 191 stumpings), as well as the single-season record of 89 dismissals in 1962. He succeeded Trevor Bailey as captain in 1967, and led Essex for seven seasons.

WEDNESDAY 20th JUNE 1866

James Burns was born in Liverpool. He played for Lancashire before joining Essex in 1887. He featured in the county's first first-class match in 1894 and also its first County Championship match, in which he scored a century. In 26 first-class matches for Essex Burns scored 713 runs at 15.50. He was also a fine footballer, and played for West Bromwich Albion and Notts County.

FRIDAY 20th JUNE 1947

Ray East was born in Manningtree. He played 405 first-class matches for Essex between 1965 and 1984, taking 1,010 wickets with his slow left-arm bowling at 25.54 and scoring 7,103 runs at 17.66. He scored one century, 113 against Hampshire in 1976. He was notorious for his humorous antics, such as when he borrowed a spectator's bicycle to transport himself between fielding positions at The Oval.

SATURDAY 20th JUNE 1998

Ronnie Irani hit a match-winning century as Essex scraped home by one wicket against Somerset at Bath. Essex were set 300 to win on the last day and slumped to 84 for 5 before Irani led a fightback with support from Robert Rollins (42) and Danny Law (46). Yet 24 were still needed when the ninth wicket fell. Last man Peter Such managed to hold up an end while Irani smashed the remaining runs, ending 127 not out.

MONDAY 21st JUNE 1982

Graham Gooch took his best first-class bowling figures of 7 for 14 against Worcestershire at Ilford. After Essex declared on 252 for 7, Gooch was introduced as first change and took full advantage of conditions that favoured swing bowling: incredibly five wickets fell without the score advancing from 25, and Worcestershire were all out for 64. Gooch then had the rare privilege of being given the new ball when Worcestershire followed on before the close. Unfortunately, no play was possible on the final day, and the match was drawn.

FRIDAY 22nd JUNE 1934

Essex beat Leicestershire in a tight finish at Chelmsford. Essex had dominated the game, but time lost on the second day meant that they only had 20 overs to make the 88 for victory in the last innings. Wickets fell regularly, but opening batsman Jim Cutmore took on the sheet-anchor role and Essex arrived at the last over with two wickets in hand and the scores level. Cutmore took a single from Alan Shipman's second ball to win the game, finishing with an invaluable 36 not out.

SUNDAY 22nd JUNE 1969

Ray East produced his career-best one-day figures of 6 for 18 from eight overs in Essex's Sunday League match against Yorkshire at Hull. Essex scored 173 for 8 from their 40 overs with Gordon Barker top-scoring with 61. East came on for the tenth over and immediately posed problems, bowling Geoff Boycott. Yorkshire were soon reduced to 68 for 7 and Keith Boyce returned to finish off the match and give Essex victory by 85 runs.

WEDNESDAY 22nd JUNE 1988

Essex recorded their largest margin of victory in a limited-overs match, beating Wiltshire by 291 runs in the first round of the NatWest Trophy at Chelmsford. They batted first and ran up 386 for 5 from their 60 overs, with contributions from Graham Gooch (70), Brian Hardie (77), Paul Prichard (77), and Derek Pringle (80 not out). No Wiltshire batsman could make much of the Essex bowling, and they limped to 95 all out with Geoff Miller taking 3 for 23.

MONDAY 22nd JUNE 1992

Essex pulled off an unlikely victory over Hampshire at Bournemouth. They were bowled out for 149 in their first innings — just two runs short of avoiding the follow-on. In their second innings they struggled to 165 for 7 — a lead of only 14 — before Mike Garnham (60) and Derek Pringle (51) added 106 for the eighth wicket. Hampshire were eventually set 160 to win, and Mark Ilott took 4 for 19 and John Childs 3 for 16 as they were bowled out for 80.

SATURDAY 22nd JUNE 2002

Essex supporters suffered a day of disappointment at Lord's as the club lost the final of the Benson and Hedges Cup to Warwickshire. Essex batted first, but their innings never really got on track: they fell to 86 for 6 before a late rally from Paul Grayson and Ashley Cowan took the total to 181 for 8. Cowan and Ronnie Irani each took an early wicket, but Ian Bell hit 65 not out and Warwickshire won with more than 13 overs to spare.

FRIDAY 23rd JUNE 1905

Essex scored a famous victory over Australia at Leyton. The match had begun inauspiciously when the county was bowled out for just 118. However, Claude Buckenham and Bert Tremlin then bowled unchanged and Australia were dismissed for 100 in 22.1 overs. Essex began the second day 51 ahead with seven second-innings wickets in hand, and extended the lead to 221. The tourists fell ten short, despite a last-wicket partnership of 45, with Buckenham and Tremlin again taking all ten wickets between them.

TUESDAY 23rd JUNE 1953

Trevor Bailey played a typically defiant innings as Essex held out for a draw against Northamptonshire at Kettering. Set 300 to win, they were deep in trouble at 39 for 4 when Bailey came out to bat. He made 81, sharing half-century stands with Doug Insole (47) and Bill Greensmith (28), and was still unbeaten at the end as Essex saw out time with nine wickets down.

TUESDAY 24th JUNE 1947

Peter Smith took 7 for 138 in the second innings against Middlesex at Colchester, the day after taking 9 for 77 in the first innings. This gave him match figures of 16 for 217 — the best by an Essex bowler in the 20th century. Smith had also scored 62 in Essex's first innings, and his efforts ensured a ten-wicket victory against a strong Middlesex side who would be crowned champions at the season's end.

TUESDAY 24th JUNE 1952

The match between Essex and Lancashire at Brentwood ended in a tie after Essex had been set 232 to win on the last afternoon. Essex came to the last over needing nine more runs to win with the last pair together. Trevor Bailey hit a six and then scrambled a two to bring the scores level with three balls remaining. Victory now seemed assured, but, rather than push a single, Bailey uncharacteristically attempted another big hit and was caught on the boundary.

TUESDAY 24th JUNE 2008

Graham Napier set a record for the highest score in English Twenty20 cricket, smashing an incredible 152 not out from only 58 balls against Sussex at Chelmsford. The innings contained ten fours and a record 16 sixes. He brought up his century from just 44 balls, and took 29 runs from the final over as Essex finished on 242 for 3. Not surprisingly, Sussex failed to get close to this total and lost by 128 runs. The innings won Napier the Walter Lawrence Trophy for the fastest century of the season with 2008 the first year when innings in limited-overs matches were eligible for this award.

SATURDAY 25th JUNE 1898

Essex beat Hampshire by 126 runs at Southampton. The whole of the second day had been lost, leaving Essex little time to force a result. They declared 226 ahead and encountered some stout defence before Charles Kortright was introduced into the attack. He took 6 for 10 to blast away the lower order, and Essex won with just 15 minutes remaining.

SATURDAY 25th JUNE 1921

Jack Russell hit a career-best 273 on the first day of the match against Northamptonshire at Leyton. He batted for four and a half hours and hit 40 fours and one six, sharing partnerships of 135 with Percy Perrin and 202 with Johnny Douglas. Essex ended the day on 465 for 5. They eventually declared on 545 for 9 and won the game by an innings and 164 runs.

WEDNESDAY 25th JUNE 1952

Colin Griffiths hit the fastest century of the season on the first day of Essex's match against Kent at Tunbridge Wells. Griffiths, whose previous top score was only 31, went in at number nine and hit 105 with two sixes and 14 fours before being stumped attempting another big hit against the leg-spinner Bill Murray-Wood. He had added 183 for the eighth wicket with Trevor Bailey (who ended the innings on 155 not out). Essex were able to declare at 456 for 8 and completed an innings victory on the following day. Griffiths celebrated his maiden — and, as it turned out, only — first-class century by flying to Paris with his girlfriend.

MONDAY 25th JUNE 1962

Barry Knight hit a career-best score of 165 as part of a dominant all-round performance against Middlesex at Brentwood. He had taken 6 for 50 on the Saturday as Middlesex were dismissed for 115. Now he produced an innings of sustained aggression featuring three sixes and 24 fours. He was ably supported by Roger Luckin (82) in a stand of 206 for the sixth wicket as Essex amassed 425 for 7 declared. When Middlesex batted again, Bill Greensmith took eight wickets to ensure that Essex completed a comfortable victory.

THURSDAY 25th JUNE 2009

Alastair Cook scored a century in Essex's Twenty20 Cup match against Surrey at The Oval. He and Mark Pettini got the Essex innings off to a superb start by adding 169 runs before Pettini was dismissed for 87 in the 17th over. Cook went on to bat right through the innings and scored exactly 100 from 57 balls, including four sixes and 11 fours. The final total of 210 for 3 proved more than enough: Graham Napier took two wickets in the second over of the Surrey reply, and Essex won by 84 runs.

FRIDAY 25th JUNE 2010

Scott Styris hit 22 off the last over to give Essex victory over Surrey in their Friends Provident Twenty20 match at Chelmsford. Surrey batted first and posted a challenging target of 187, with Steven Davies hitting 89 from 50 balls. Essex had struggled to 28 for 2 after 5 overs when Styris came in. The New Zealander reached 50 from 32 balls, but 22 were still needed from the last six balls. Styris only needed five: he hit Andrew Symonds for four, six, two, four, and six to win the match. This left him undefeated on 106 from 50 balls, with eight sixes and six fours.

SATURDAY 26th JUNE 1920

Dick Horsfall was born in Todmorden, Yorkshire. He played 207 first-class matches for Essex between 1947 and 1955, scoring 9,583 runs at an average of 29.59. He hit 17 centuries for the county, with a highest score of 206 against Kent at Blackheath in 1951. After leaving Essex he played briefly for Glamorgan before injuries forced him to retire. He died in Halifax in 1981 at the age of 61.

WEDNESDAY 26th JUNE 1935

Hopper Read took a hat-trick on the first day of Essex's match against Gloucestershire at Bristol. He had William Neale caught behind for 80 and then bowled the last two batsmen, Tom Goddard and Harry Smith, to wrap up the Gloucestershire first innings for 163. He also took 6 for 38 in the second innings as Essex won by nine wickets.

FRIDAY 26th JUNE 1992

Mark Waugh and Nasser Hussain put together an unbeaten partnership of 347 against Lancashire at Ilford, setting a new county record for the third wicket. Waugh hit 219 — his highest score for the county — and Hussain 172, as Essex reached 510 for 2 from only 97.1 overs before declaring. Essex did not have to bat again, as John Childs and Peter Such bowled Lancashire out twice, earning an innings victory inside two days.

SUNDAY 26th JUNE 2011

Adam Wheater and James Foster set a county record for the sixth wicket, adding 253 against Northamptonshire at Chelmsford. Until this stand the match had been a low-scoring affair, 25 wickets falling while 345 runs were scored. Indeed, Essex were in some trouble at 63 for 5 in their second innings, but Wheater hit 164 from 143 balls, with four sixes and 18 fours, while Foster contributed 103 from 155 balls with 13 fours. Northamptonshire were set 416 to win and lost by 171 runs.

MONDAY 27th JUNE 1960

Essex bowled out Leicestershire twice in a day to secure an innings victory at Hinckley. Defending a modest score of 263 for 9 declared, they engineered a remarkable collapse in the Leicestershire first innings as the last six wickets fell without a run being added. Four of these fell to Paddy Phelan, who took 5 for 33. Essex enforced the follow-on and there was another collapse in the second innings as the hosts fell from 78 for 2 to 127 all out. Phelan took 4 for 68 but was surpassed this time by Ken Preston, who finished with 5 for 26.

MONDAY 27th JUNE 1977

Ken McEwan scored a career-best 218 against Sussex at Chelmsford. He shared a partnership of 258 for the fourth wicket with Keith Fletcher (70), which rescued Essex from trouble at 12 for 3. Essex established a lead of 108, but the match was drawn. McEwan would continue in this rich vein of form with scores of 102, 104 (in a Sunday League match), 116, and 106 not out in his next four innings.

TUESDAY 27th JUNE 1995

Graham Gooch took remarkable figures of 5 for 8 in 2.4 overs in Essex's NatWest Trophy first-round match against Cheshire at Chester. Gooch came on towards the end with Cheshire already hopelessly adrift of Essex's score of 265 for 8. He immediately broke a stubborn 89-run partnership between Jonathan Gray and Richard Hignett, bowling both batsmen. The remaining wickets tumbled in quick succession as Cheshire subsided from 185 for 4 to 201 all out.

MONDAY 28th JUNE 1886

Cecil "Pickles" Douglas was born in Clapton. He played 21 first-class matches for Essex between 1912 and 1919, scoring 326 runs at an average of 12.07. He was the brother of Essex captain Johnny Douglas, but there was no hint of nepotism in their relations: Johnny dropped his brother down the batting order despite a couple of useful performances, which led to the latter's premature retirement from cricket to pursue a highly successful career as a boxing referee. He died in Frinton in 1954 at the age of 68.

SATURDAY 29th JUNE 2002

Essex successfully chased 381 in 80 overs on the last afternoon to beat Gloucestershire by three wickets at Archdeacon Meadow. Darren Robinson and Will Jefferson got the innings off to a solid start with a stand of 111. Robinson and Aftab Habib then added 180 for the second wicket, and after Habib was out for 82, the Essex middle-order batsmen were able to accelerate towards victory, with Graham Napier hitting two sixes in a quickfire 20. Stand-in captain Robinson was seventh out for a fine 175, but Jonathan Dakin and John Stephenson saw Essex home with seven balls to spare.

SUNDAY 30th JUNE 1935

Les Savill was born in Brentwood. He played 125 first-class matches for the county between 1953 and 1961, scoring 3,919 runs at an average of 21.29 including four centuries. His best season was 1959, when he was promoted to open the batting and passed 1,000 runs for the only time. However, he failed to sustain this form and was released two years later.

TUESDAY 30th JUNE 1953

Trevor Bailey played a career-defining innings, holding the Australian bowlers at bay for over four hours in the second Ashes Test at Lord's. He joined Willie Watson on the last morning of the match with England in trouble on 73 for 4 and the two shared in the famous 'backs-to-the-wall' stand, tenaciously blocking all of the bowlers and seeing off an assault from Lindwall and Miller when the new ball was taken. In the course of the day Bailey ground his way to 71 and Watson made 109. Both batsmen were dismissed in the final hour, but the Test match was saved and England would go on to regain the Ashes with a win at The Oval.

MONDAY 30th JUNE 1980

Ryan ten Doeschate was born in Port Elizabeth, South Africa. He played his early cricket in South Africa's Western Province and made his debut for Essex in 2003, qualifying as a Kolpak player by virtue of holding a Dutch passport. He soon established himself as a hard-hitting batsman and useful medium-pace bowler. By the end of the 2011 season he had played 82 first-class matches for the county, scoring 4,166 runs at 38.93 (including 11 centuries) and taking 143 wickets at an average of 34.76. He represented the Netherlands at the World Cup in 2007 and 2011 (hitting two centuries in the latter tournament) and at the ICC World Twenty20 in 2009 (when he saw his side to a famous victory over England). He has also played Twenty20 cricket for the Kolkata Knight Riders in the Indian Premier League.

ESSEX CCC
On This Day

JULY

TUESDAY 1st JULY 1941

Arthur Heatley died in Brentwood at the age of 75. He was born in Brighton and played one first-class match for Essex against Yorkshire at Halifax in 1894 — the club's inaugural first-class season. He scored seven and 13 not out and bowled one over for ten runs. However, he did take four catches for a side that was notoriously poor in the field. Essex lost the match by seven wickets.

WEDNESDAY 2nd JULY 1986

Alfred Grimwood died in Chingford at the age of 80. He was a Walthamstow-born left-hander who played four first-class matches for the county in 1925, scoring 26 runs at 4.33 and bowling a single over at a cost of five runs.

SUNDAY 3rd JULY 1983

Ken McEwan and Graham Gooch put on 273 for the second wicket in the John Player League match against Nottinghamshire at Trent Bridge. The partnership remains a county record for any wicket in a limited-overs match, and the Essex total of 306 for 2 was the second-highest achieved by the county in the history of the 40-over competition. McEwan finished unbeaten on 162 — his highest one-day score — while Gooch was out just before the end of the innings for 116. Among the Nottinghamshire bowlers on the receiving end of this awesome display was a 19-year-old Peter Such. Derek Randall scored a century for Nottinghamshire in reply, but Essex won easily by 89 runs.

WEDNESDAY 4th JULY 1900

Walter Mead achieved his best figures in first-class cricket, taking 9 for 40 on the last day of a rain-affected draw against Hampshire at Southampton. He bowled 32.3 overs unchanged on the second evening and — after a long delay for rain — the third afternoon, as Hampshire were all out for 131 in their first innings. Unfortunately, there was no time for Essex to force a victory, although Mead did complete ten wickets in the match. It was the third time that Mead had taken nine wickets in an innings, and he also took eight wickets in an innings on five occasions.

WEDNESDAY 4th JULY 1979

Essex beat Yorkshire by three wickets at Chelmsford in the semi-final of the Benson and Hedges Cup to advance to their first Lord's final. Yorkshire were restricted to 173 for 9 despite an opening stand of 107. The match was in the balance when Essex fell to 112 for 5, but Keith Pont made a steady 36 to see them within five runs of victory before Neil Smith came in to hit the winning runs against his former county.

FRIDAY 5th JULY 1991

Saleem Malik and Nasser Hussain put on a county-record fourth-wicket partnership of 314 against Surrey at The Oval. The pair came together with the score on 9 for 3, but Hussain made 128 and Malik 185 not out, allowing Essex to declare on 338 for 5. Essex would go on to lose the match, with Alec Stewart playing a match-winning innings for Surrey on the last day.

SATURDAY 5th JULY 2008

Essex beat Yorkshire at Chelmsford in the semi-final of the Friends Provident Trophy. Alastair Cook top-scored for Essex with 95 from 127 balls, but Graham Napier took the man of the match award with an innings of 61 from 34 balls, including six sixes. This took Essex to 285 for 8 from their 50 overs. Facing this stiff challenge, Yorkshire reached 140 for 1 but then collapsed to 198 all out. Ryan ten Doeschate and Danish Kaneria took three wickets each as Essex progressed to Lord's.

MONDAY 6th JULY 1863

Tom Russell was born in Lewisham. He was Essex's regular wicketkeeper in their earliest years in first-class cricket, playing 162 matches between 1894 and 1905. He took 246 catches and 88 stumpings, and scored 3,106 runs at an average of 15.45. Those runs included three centuries, with a highest score of 139 against Derbyshire in 1900. The Russell family made a significant contribution to Essex cricket: Tom was succeeded behind the stumps by his brother Edward, while his son Jack Russell would become one of the club's greatest ever batsmen.

FRIDAY 7th JULY 1916

Frank Street died at Ovillers-la-Boisselle in the Somme aged 46. He was serving as a lieutenant in the Royal Fusiliers when he was killed by a sniper. Street had been born in Kensington and played nine first-class matches for Essex in 1898 and 1899, scoring 246 runs at 22.36, with a top score of 76 against Leicestershire in his final match.

SATURDAY 8th JULY 1911

Ken Farnes, one of Essex's greatest bowlers, was born in Leytonstone. He played 79 first-class matches for the county between 1930 and 1939, his appearances limited first by his studies at Cambridge University and later by his job as a teacher at Worksop College in Nottinghamshire. He took 367 wickets for the county at an average of 19.30 with a best performance of 8 for 38 against Glamorgan in 1938. Farnes was one of *Wisden's* Cricketers of the Year for 1939, and played 15 Test matches for England, taking 60 wickets at 28.65. He died in a plane crash in 1941.

FRIDAY 8th JULY 2011

Tim Southee took 6 for 16 against Glamorgan at Chelmsford, setting a record for the best figures by an Essex bowler in a Twenty20 match. Most of the damage was done in his final over when he took four wickets, including a hat-trick as Nick James, Stewart Walters, and Alex Jones were dismissed from consecutive balls. Essex restricted Glamorgan to 144 for 9 and won the match by five wickets.

SATURDAY 9th JULY 1898

Gloucestershire beat Essex by one wicket in a controversial match at Leyton. There was bad feeling between the sides after Gloucestershire claimed two dubious catches and then WG Grace appeared to intimidate the umpire into reversing his decision after he had been given out. As Gloucestershire closed in on victory, Charles Kortright subjected Grace to a fearsome attack, and when the umpire declined two strong appeals Kortright left nothing to doubt by removing Grace's middle stump. However, Grace's innings of 49 proved sufficient to help his side achieve a narrow win.

FRIDAY 9th JULY 1937

Essex recorded one of their most comprehensive victories, beating Northamptonshire by an innings and 293 runs at Colchester. Essex batted first and scored 588 for 9 declared, with centuries from Reg Taylor, Jack O'Connor, and Stan Nichols. Taylor and O'Connor added 333 for the third wicket, a new county record for any wicket. The visitors were bowled out for 169 and 126, leg-spinner Peter Smith taking 7 for 56 and 6 for 62.

THURSDAY 9th JULY 1992

Essex beat Lancashire by one wicket in the second round of the NatWest Trophy at Chelmsford. A win seemed far from likely after Lancashire posted a score of 318 for 8 — the highest total ever conceded by the county in a one-day match. Graham Gooch and John Stephenson put on 123 for the first wicket, but Essex were still 90 runs behind when the eighth wicket fell. Mike Garnham then produced a heroic innings, aided first by Don Topley and then by John Childs, hitting 53 from 37 balls and winning the match by hitting the penultimate ball for four.

MONDAY 9th JULY 2007

Essex piled up an enormous 700 for 9 against Nottinghamshire at Chelmsford. James Foster scored 204 and shared in partnerships of 254 for the seventh wicket with Andy Bichel (148) and 195 for the eighth wicket with Graham Napier (125, including eight sixes). Yet this total would be passed by Nottinghamshire, who made the most of the benign conditions to score 791 as the match ended in a draw.

MONDAY 10th JULY 1972

Essex took the field for the start of their game against Kent at Maidstone without injured captain Brian Taylor. It was the first time since May 1961 that Taylor had missed a first-class game — a streak of 301 consecutive appearances. This remains a county record, and is unlikely to be broken in the era of four-day matches. Richard Baker made his debut as Taylor's replacement behind the stumps, but the loss of the first day to rain turned the match into a dull draw.

FRIDAY 11th JULY 1913

Wicketkeeper-batsman Paul Gibb was born in York. He had played for Yorkshire and Cambridge University and won eight England caps either side of World War Two, but he had been out of first-class cricket for four years when he was brought to Essex at the age of 38 to replace Tom Wade. He played 145 first-class matches for the county between 1951 and 1956, scoring 6,328 runs at 26.58 with eight centuries. He also took 273 catches and made 63 stumpings. After retiring as a player he spent ten years as an umpire.

SUNDAY 11th JULY 1971

Keith Boyce took a hat-trick in the John Player League game against Somerset at Westcliff-on-Sea. The match was reduced to 39 overs per side, and Boyce took wickets with the last three balls of the final over of the Somerset innings, having Peter Robinson caught behind and bowling Hallam Moseley and Derek Taylor. He ended with figures of 4 for 36, but Essex lost the match by 11 runs.

FRIDAY 11th JULY 1975

Graham Gooch endured a painful Test debut against Australia at Edgbaston. Coming in at number five, he was caught behind off the bowling of Max Walker for nought from his third ball. He would make another duck in the second innings as England lost the game heavily. He was dropped after one more match, and it was another three years before he got his next chance, but he went on to score more Test runs than any other Englishman.

TUESDAY 11th JULY 2006

Ronnie Irani became the first player to score a century for Essex in a Twenty20 match as the county beat Sussex by four wickets at Hove. Sussex had posted a challenging score of 173, with Matt Prior hitting 73 from 44 balls. Skipper Irani countered with 100 not out from 61 balls, including 13 fours and two sixes. The match went into the final over, and Irani hit the last ball for four to win the match and bring up his own hundred at the same time.

RAVI BOPARA HIT A T20 TON IN JULY 2010 – SEE OVER

SUNDAY 11th JULY 2010

Ravi Bopara scored an unbeaten 105 in Essex's Friends Provident Twenty20 match against Somerset at Chelmsford. His runs came in 62 balls and included eight fours and six sixes as he batted right through the innings of 173 for 6. Not content, he also took two wickets when Somerset batted, but the visitors won with five balls in hand.

FRIDAY 12th JULY 1895

Essex scored 692 — their highest score at the time — against Somerset at Taunton. The innings contained centuries from Bob Carpenter (153), Charlie McGahey (147), and Bunny Lucas (135), while wicketkeeper Tom Russell hit 99. The size of the total was especially surprising as at the time the county was considered to be strong in bowling but weak in batting. Over a century later, the score remains the highest ever recorded by Essex in an away fixture.

SUNDAY 12th JULY 1998

Essex won the Benson and Hedges Cup for the second time, beating Leicestershire in a one-sided final at Lord's. The match took place over two days, with Essex posting 268 for 7 from their 50 overs on the Saturday thanks to a second-wicket partnership of 134 between Paul Prichard (92) and Nasser Hussain (88). There was then a delay for rain, and when the Leicestershire innings finally began on the Sunday afternoon Ashley Cowan took three early wickets and Mark Ilott produced a spell of 3 for 10 from eight overs. Leicestershire were bowled out for 76, the lowest score in a Benson and Hedges Cup Final, and Essex won by 192 runs.

SATURDAY 13th JULY 1895

Essex completed victory over Somerset at Taunton by an innings and 317 runs — still their largest margin of victory in a first-class match. The victory was based on the huge score of 692 that they had compiled on the previous day, giving them a first-innings lead of 446. Somerset began the last day on 38 for 1 and were bowled out before lunch for 129 with Charles Kortright taking seven wickets and Walter Mead three.

SATURDAY 14th JULY 1917

Frank Vigar was born in Bruton, Somerset. He played 256 first-class matches for Essex between 1938 and 1954, scoring 8,660 runs at 25.85 and taking 241 wickets with his leg breaks at an average of 37.90. He scored 11 centuries, with a top score of 144 against Northamptonshire in 1950, and is remembered especially for sharing with Peter Smith in the county's record last-wicket partnership of 218 against Derbyshire in 1947. He died in Hampshire in 2004 at the age of 86.

WEDNESDAY 14th JULY 1976

Essex suffered probably the most embarrassing result in the county's history, losing to Minor Counties side Hertfordshire at Hitchin in the second round of the Gillette Cup. Hertfordshire were bowled out for 153, Ray East taking 4 for 28, and Essex appeared to be on course for a comfortable win as they reached 71 for 1 in reply, but on a turning pitch they collapsed against the spin of Dilip Doshi and Robin Johns and were all out for 120.

SATURDAY 15th JULY 1989

Essex lost an exciting Benson and Hedges Cup Final against Nottinghamshire off the last ball at Lord's. Alan Lilley scored 95 as Essex posted a total of 243 for 7 from their 55 overs. Nottinghamshire remained in the hunt thanks to an innings of 86 from Tim Robinson, but still needed nine from the last over. John Lever restricted them to five from the first five balls, but Eddie Hemmings hit the last ball of the match for four to deny Essex the trophy.

THURSDAY 16th JULY 1931

Stan Nichols took a hat-trick in Essex's match against Yorkshire at Headingley. Essex had been bowled out for 108, and Yorkshire reached 87 for 4 in reply, but Nichols bowled Wilf Barber, had Emmott Robinson caught at the wicket, and bowled Arthur Wood to peg back the hosts. Nichols finished with 6 for 26 and the Yorkshire lead was restricted to a single run. However, Essex were bowled out cheaply again in their second innings and lost by ten wickets.

WEDNESDAY 16th JULY 1952

Ken McEwan was born in Bedford, in South Africa's Eastern Cape. He played 282 first-class matches for Essex between 1974 and 1985, and had a major role in a period of sustained success, scoring 18,088 runs at an average of 43.37. He hit 52 centuries and passed 1,000 runs in each of his 12 seasons with the club. He was named as one of *Wisden's* Cricketers of the Year in 1978, but his finest season was probably 1983, when he scored 2,051 runs at 68.36 to help Essex win the championship and was the Professional Cricketers' Association Player of the Year.

THURSDAY 17th JULY 1958

Trevor Bailey took 8 for 29 — his second-best figures for Essex — against Derbyshire at Westcliff-on-Sea. Bailey and Ken Preston bowled unchanged through Derbyshire's first innings, dismissing the visitors for 72. However, Essex fared little better on a difficult pitch: they were out for 127 and 106, and Derbyshire managed to make 162 in the last innings to win by two wickets.

SUNDAY 17th JULY 1983

Essex scored their highest total in the John Player League, 310 for 5 against Glamorgan at Southend. Graham Gooch led the way with 176, the highest score by an Essex player in a 40-over match, while Derek Pringle weighed in with 52. The total was more than any other team had previously scored in the competition and, although Javed Miandad and Rodney Ontong hit 50s for Glamorgan, Essex won by 56 runs.

TUESDAY 17th JULY 1984

John Lever took career-best figures of 8 for 37 against Gloucestershire at Bristol. The wicket had presented no problems in the first innings of the match as both sides reached 300 with comfort. However, Lever and Neil Foster soon reduced Gloucestershire to 21 for 5 in their second innings. There was a brief rally before Lever took the last five wickets in short order on the last morning. Gloucestershire were all out for 90, and Essex won by eight wickets to take another step towards a successful defence of their County Championship title.

SUNDAY 18th JULY 1943

All-rounder Stuart Turner was born in Chester. One of the great Essex servants, he played 354 first-class matches between 1965 and 1986, scoring 9,264 runs at 22.87 and taking 810 wickets at an average of 25.90. He hit four centuries, with a top score of 121 against Somerset in 1970, while his best bowling figures were 6 for 26 against Northamptonshire in 1977. Turner later played Minor Counties cricket for Cambridgeshire.

FRIDAY 19th JULY 1889

Hugh Owen became the first player to make a century for the club against another county side, carrying his bat for 153 against Leicestershire at Leyton. He batted for 143.1 five-ball overs as Essex scored 295. Harry Pickett then took 7 for 15 (giving him match figures of 11 for 35) as Leicestershire were bowled out for 51 and Essex won by an innings and 123 runs.

TUESDAY 19th JULY 1904

Percy Perrin scored the only triple-century ever recorded by an Essex player, against Derbyshire at Chesterfield. His 343 not out included 68 fours, which remains a world record, as Essex reached 597. As with so many outstanding individual feats by Essex players, it was not accompanied by a victory. The county was bowled out for 97 in its second innings — there is a suggestion that Perrin's feat may have been celebrated excessively by his team-mates — and lost the match by nine wickets. Perrin's score remains the highest by any player on a losing side.

MONDAY 19th JULY 1920

Jack Russell orchestrated an unlikely comeback on the second day against Middlesex at Lord's. Middlesex had scored 446 and reduced Essex to 184 for 8 when Russell was joined by Laurie Eastman, who was playing only his third first-class match. By the close the two had shared a stand of 175 for the ninth wicket. Russell finished the day unbeaten on 192, while Eastman had reached 87. The stand was extended to 184 on the following day — then a county record for the ninth wicket — and Essex escaped with a draw.

WEDNESDAY 19th JULY 1972

John Lever and Keith Boyce destroyed Middlesex with five wickets each in the Gillette Cup second round match at Westcliff-on-Sea. The pair bowled unchanged and dismissed the visitors in 19.4 overs for a competition-record low of 41, Boyce taking 5 for 22 and Lever 5 for 8. Essex won by eight wickets, but would be eliminated in the next round.

SATURDAY 20th JULY 1985

Essex lost the final of the Benson and Hedges Cup to Leicestershire at Lord's. Essex batted first and were restricted to 213 for 8 from their 55 overs, Graham Gooch top-scoring with 57. They reduced their opponents to 135 for 5, but were thwarted by an unbroken sixth-wicket partnership of 80 between Peter Willey and future Essex player Mike Garnham, as Leicestershire won with three overs to spare.

WEDNESDAY 21st JULY 1948

Ray Smith hit his maiden first-class century against Derbyshire at Colchester. He came in at number nine after Dusty Rhodes had taken a hat-trick and hit 112 out of a partnership of 152 with Frank Vigar, helping Essex to reach 446. Smith's innings was the fastest hundred of the season — the first of three times that the big-hitting all-rounder would achieve this distinction. He also took six wickets in the match, while his cousin Peter Smith took 10 for 174, as Essex won by an innings and 44 runs.

SATURDAY 21st JULY 1979

Over a century after the club's formation, Essex finally won their first trophy, capturing the Benson and Hedges Cup after beating Surrey by 35 runs. Playing in their first ever Lord's final, Essex were put in to bat and scored a then-record 290 for 6 from 55 overs. Graham Gooch became the first player to score a century in a Benson and Hedges Cup Final, making 120 and putting on 124 for the second wicket with Ken McEwan, who scored 72. The Surrey reply featured half-centuries from Geoff Howarth and Roger Knight, but Essex took wickets regularly and bowled out their opponents for 255 to complete a 35-run victory.

MONDAY 21st JULY 1980

Exactly one year after winning the trophy, Essex tasted defeat in the final of the Benson and Hedges Cup against Northamptonshire. After a washout on the Saturday, Essex restricted their opponents to 209, with Allan Lamb scoring 72. Graham Gooch got the reply off to a good start with 60 before the innings became bogged down against the Northamptonshire spinners. Ten runs were needed from the last over, but the tail-enders could not make much of Sarfraz Nawaz and Essex lost by six runs.

TUESDAY 22nd JULY 1952

Essex survived a scare to beat Glamorgan by one wicket at Westcliff-on-Sea. Chasing an apparently simple 86, they reached 62 for 1 before Don Shepherd and Ken Lewis took eight wickets for just 19 runs. Five were still needed when Frank Vigar was joined by the last man Charles Kenny. The pair ran a leg-bye before Vigar hit a four to win the match.

SATURDAY 23rd JULY 1921

George Louden took a hat-trick against Somerset at Southend. His victims were the tail-enders Robertson-Glasgow, Bridges and Amor, as the visitors were dismissed for 163 with Louden claiming 6 for 54. Essex would take a first-innings lead of 83, but still contrived to lose by 65 runs.

THURSDAY 23rd JULY 1953

Graham Gooch was born in Whipps Cross. Essex's most prolific batsman of all time, he played 391 first-class matches for the county between 1973 and 1997, scoring 30,701 runs at 51.77, including 94 centuries, while his medium-pace bowling brought him 200 wickets at an average of 32.70. He is also the county's leading run-scorer in one-day cricket with 16,536 runs at 40.93, including 34 centuries. He captained Essex between 1986 and 1994 (although Keith Fletcher took over for the 1988 season), and served as the county's coach from 2001 to 2005. Besides holding numerous county records, he scored a record 8,900 runs for England in 118 Test matches and made 4,290 runs in 125 one-day internationals. No player in the history of cricket has scored more runs in all forms of the game.

SATURDAY 23rd JULY 1983

Essex lost to Middlesex by four runs in the Benson and Hedges Cup Final at Lord's. Middlesex made a moderate 196, with Neil Foster recording the excellent figures of 3 for 26 from his 11 overs. Graham Gooch, on his 30th birthday, then got the reply off to a flying start with 46 from 51 balls, and the county appeared set for victory at 127 for 1. However, none of the middle-order managed to establish themselves, and after a late rush of wickets Essex were all out for 192 from the first ball of the final over.

SATURDAY 24th JULY 1897

Essex beat Yorkshire by one run at Huddersfield in a close-fought encounter. Essex had led by five runs after the first innings, and recovered from 51 for 5 to score 294 in their second innings thanks to a maiden century from Johnny Turner. On the last day, four Yorkshiremen scored 50s, taking the home side to 283 for 7 — just 15 behind — before George Hirst was run out for 54. Walter Mead then prised out the last two batsmen to give Essex the narrowest of wins.

WEDNESDAY 24th JULY 1907

Sailor Young took a hat-trick on the last day of Essex's match against Leicestershire at Leyton. He trapped Knight leg-before-wicket, bowled Coe, and then had Crawford caught behind. He finished the innings with figures of 4 for 6 from five overs as Leicestershire were dismissed for 91. However, the effort was to no avail as the rain-affected match ended in a draw.

THURSDAY 24th JULY 1947

Off-spinner David Acfield was born in Chelmsford. He made his first-class debut in 1966 for Cambridge University and played 378 first-class matches for Essex between 1966 and 1986, taking 855 wickets at an average of 27.49, with a best performance of 8 for 55 against Kent in 1981. Acfield was also an accomplished fencer: he was a member of the English men's sabre team that won gold at the 1970 Commonwealth Games and also competed at the Olympic Games in 1968 and 1972.

TUESDAY 25th JULY 1893

Fred Nicholas was born in Malaysia. He was an Oxford Blue at football and athletics and played 63 first-class matches for Essex between 1912 and 1929, scoring 2,255 runs at 22.77. His only century was an innings of 140 in a defeat against Surrey at Leyton in 1926. His grandson Mark Nicholas was captain of Hampshire and became a well-known television presenter.

SUNDAY 26th JULY 1903

Leonard Crawley was born in Nacton, Suffolk. He was a fine amateur batsman who played for Worcestershire and Cambridge University before joining Essex in 1926. His other interests meant that he was unable to turn out for the county on a regular basis, and he appeared in only 56 first-class matches between 1926 and 1936, scoring 2,949 runs at 33.89 with six centuries, including a highest score of 222 against Glamorgan in 1928. Crawley was an excellent golfer, winning the English amateur championship in 1931 and representing Great Britain in the Walker Cup on four occasions. He was later the golf correspondent of the *Daily Telegraph*.

SATURDAY 27th JULY 1895

Walter Mead took 9 for 52 in the second innings of Essex's match against Hampshire at Southampton. He had also taken 8 for 67 in the first innings, and his match figures of 17 for 119 established a county record that still stands. Six of Mead's second-innings victims were bowled as Hampshire were all out for 136. But this still left Essex a target of 255, and the batsmen were unequal to the task, all out for 83 to lose by 171 runs.

FRIDAY 27th JULY 1900

Charlie McGahey and Percy Perrin, known as "the Essex twins", put on 323 for the third wicket against Kent at Leyton. It was the first time that an Essex pair had shared a triple-century stand, and would be a county record until 1937. Perrin was the major contributor with 205, including 22 fours, while McGahey made 142, including 14 fours. Essex reached 551, but Kent, assisted by some bad weather, were able to escape with a draw.

TUESDAY 27th JULY 1920

Essex beat Middlesex in a pulsating finish at Leyton. Essex had started badly, 24 for 4 on the first morning before eventually reaching 133. They conceded a first-innings lead of 79 and then managed only 196 in their second innings. Middlesex needed 118 to win, but the match became a personal triumph for Johnny Douglas, who single-handedly reduced them to 33 for 6 and then came back to finish the innings by bowling top-scorer Plum Warner. Douglas finished with 7 for 47 as Essex won by four runs.

FRIDAY 27th JULY 1923

Henry Franklin scored a century after coming in at number ten to save the follow-on and ensure a draw for Essex against Middlesex at Leyton. Middlesex had declared on 489 for 6 and reduced Essex to 216 for 8 when Franklin joined Johnny Douglas. Franklin, whose previous highest score was 53, proceeded to hit 106, sharing with Douglas in a ninth-wicket stand of 160, as Essex reached safety with a total of 404. Franklin was a student at Oxford at the time, and played as an amateur for Essex until 1931, captaining the side on several occasions.

SATURDAY 27th JULY 1985

Wicketkeeper David East celebrated his 26th birthday by setting a county record — and equalling a world record — with eight catches in an innings against Somerset at Taunton. East accounted for the first eight Somerset batsmen to be dismissed, before Colin Dredge was bowled. Ian Botham — who had hit 152 before becoming one of East's victims — then declared with nine wickets down to deny East the possibility of a ninth catch. Essex eventually won the rain-interrupted match thanks to an unbeaten 173 from Graham Gooch.

FRIDAY 27th JULY 1990

Graham Gooch reached the highest score of his career, 333 for England against India at Lord's. His innings contained 43 fours and three sixes, and was the third highest ever recorded by an England batsman. He also scored a century in the second innings to give him a match aggregate of 456 runs, still a Test record.

TUESDAY 27th JULY 2010

Essex gained a thrilling victory over Lancashire in their quarter-final encounter in the Friends Provident Twenty20 Cup at Chelmsford. Lancashire posted a challenging 183 for 6 from their 20 overs, and Essex lost Ravi Bopara early before a stand of 147 between Mark Pettini and Matt Walker got the innings on track. Twenty runs were still needed from two overs when Pettini was out for 81, but skipper James Foster came in and hit three consecutive boundaries against his opposite number Glen Chapple. Matt Walker (74 not out) then ended things from the first ball of the final over.

MONDAY 28th JULY 2008

Ravi Bopara produced a superb all-round performance in Essex's NatWest Pro40 win over Derbyshire. He hit 112 from only 59 balls, with seven sixes and nine fours, three of his sixes going out of the Derby ground. This whirlwind innings overshadowed a more orthodox 108 not out from Jason Gallian as Essex piled up 304 for 1. Derbyshire made a strong reply in batter-friendly conditions, but Bopara took 4 for 52 as Essex won by 25 runs.

SATURDAY 29th JULY 2006

Andy Flower scored a career-best 271 not out against Northamptonshire at Northampton. The innings occupied ten and a half hours, spread over three days, and featured a six and 37 fours. It was made in a defensive context after Northamptonshire had scored 660 in their first innings. Essex faced a likely follow-on at 248 for 5, but Flower shared in century stands with James Foster (60), Tim Phillips (46), and Andy Bichel (74) and saw his side to safety as the county reached a total of 620.

FRIDAY 29th JULY 2011

David Masters took 8 for 10 to bowl Essex to victory against Leicestershire at Southend. Essex had set their opponents a victory target of 315 after a century from Ravi Bopara, but Masters took a wicket with his third ball and then took three wickets in his fourth over to reduce Leicestershire to 10 for 5. There was no recovery and they were bowled out for 34 in just 14.4 overs.

MONDAY 30th JULY 1951

Paul Gibb and Dick Horsfall shared a third-wicket stand of 343 against Kent at Blackheath. Gibb hit 141 and Horsfall a career-best 206 as the pair set a new county record for any wicket that would stand until 1990. The fine batting of the first innings proved to be in stark contrast to a shambolic effort in the second innings, when Essex were left with only 17 overs to chase 126: they fell to 9 for 7 before Sonny Avery and Frank Vigar batted out time.

WEDNESDAY 30th JULY 1980

Essex lost their Gillette Cup quarter-final against Surrey at Chelmsford by the narrowest possible margin, having lost more wickets with the scores tied. Surrey scored 195 for 7, and Essex fell to 35 for 4 before Brian Hardie led a recovery with a score of 70. He and Norbert Phillip appeared to be steering Essex to victory with a stand of 77, but both were out in quick succession, and Ray East was run out in the last over while going for the winning run.

WEDNESDAY 31st JULY 1935

Essex bowled out Yorkshire for 31 at Huddersfield, with Stan Nichols taking 4 for 17 and Hopper Read 6 for 11. Nichols then scored a fine century as Essex took a lead of 303, and took a further seven wickets as Essex completed an innings victory on the following morning. It was the only match that Yorkshire lost all season, and the decisive victory was all the sweeter for the fresh memories of the record stand of 555 that Yorkshire's Holmes and Sutcliffe had scored against Essex three years earlier.

THURSDAY 31st JULY 2003

James Middlebrook took a hat-trick on the second day of Essex's match against Kent at Canterbury. He had Martin Saggers leg-before-wicket with the last ball of his 30th over and then dismissed Muttiah Muralitharan and Alamgir Sheriyar with the first two balls of his 31st to end the Kent second innings. Middlebrook's hat-trick left Essex needing 291 to win, but they lost by 55 runs.

ESSEX CCC
On This Day

AUGUST

THURSDAY 1st AUGUST 1907

John William Arthur "Stevie" Stephenson was born in Hong Kong. He was a career soldier who played his earliest first-class cricket in India before appearing in 61 matches for Essex between 1934 and 1939. He took 174 wickets at an average of 23.88 and scored 1,050 runs at 14.58. Stephenson was noted for his manic enthusiasm in the field and served successfully as co-captain in 1939. During the Second World War he was awarded the Distinguished Service Order for his actions in Tunisia. He died in Pulborough, Sussex, in 1982 at the age of 74.

SATURDAY 1st AUGUST 1925

Jack O'Connor — better known as one of Essex's greatest batsmen — took a hat-trick with his leg-breaks against Worcestershire. He bowled brothers Maurice and Henry Foster and then caught and bowled Gilbert Ashton to reduce the opposition to 107 for 5, and finished with 5 for 40 as Worcestershire made 241. The match was later interrupted by bad weather and ended drawn.

FRIDAY 2nd AUGUST 1912

Walter Gordon "Don" Spencer was born in Chingford. He played two first-class matches in 1938 and another in 1948, scoring 52 runs at 13.00 and taking one wicket for eight runs. He was a fine club cricketer and captained the Essex second XI in the early 1950s. He died in Chelmsford in 1971 at the age of 58.

THURSDAY 3rd AUGUST 1893

Walter Mead took 9 for 136 as Essex put up a strong showing in their first encounter with an Australian touring side, bowling them out for 250. Mead would bowl unchanged through both of Australia's innings, clocking up 72.4 five-ball overs and taking match figures of 17 for 205 as Essex had the better of a drawn game. The match was not accorded first-class status, but this fine performance helped Essex to achieve the accolade the following year. Two years later Mead repeated the feat of taking 17 wickets — this time in a first-class fixture — and he remains the only Essex bowler to have taken so many in a match.

TUESDAY 4th AUGUST 1914

Bert Tremlin took a hat-trick as Essex bowled out Derbyshire for a paltry 31 at Derby. Johnny Douglas had already taken four quick wickets before Tremlin dismissed Slater, Baggallay, and Forrester to leave Derbyshire in tatters at 26 for 7. Tremlin finished with 4 for 6 while Douglas took 6 for 21. Tremlin then took 6 for 43 when Derbyshire followed on as Essex won the match inside two days by an innings and 131 runs.

THURSDAY 4th AUGUST 1988

Graham Gooch captained England for the first time in the final Test against the West Indies at The Oval. Gooch was the fourth England captain of a turbulent summer in which the series was lost 4-0. He appeared a reluctant choice, but he would go on to lead England in 34 Tests. The England side included an unprecedented four Essex players — Gooch, Derek Pringle, Neil Foster, and John Childs — but they would lose by eight wickets.

FRIDAY 4th AUGUST 1995

Essex reached 662 for 7 before declaring against Hampshire at Colchester. The Essex total was the sixth highest in the club's history and featured centuries from Graham Gooch (142), Nasser Hussain (145), and Mark Waugh (136), as well as significant contributions from Ronnie Irani (78) and Robert Rollins (85). Essex then turned the game over to the spin bowlers Peter Such and John Childs, who took 19 wickets between them as the county won by an innings and 254 runs.

MONDAY 4th AUGUST 1997

Peter Such came off the pitch a tired man after the Leicestershire innings of 515 for 9 at Colchester. The innings had lasted a marathon 210 overs, of which Such had bowled 86, the most by any Essex player in a single innings. A remarkable 49 of those 86 overs were maidens as Such took 4 for 94. He had taken two early wickets, after which he became engaged in an attritional struggle as Leicestershire, replying to Essex's 533, kept him out to force a draw.

WEDNESDAY 5th AUGUST 1981

Essex beat Sussex by 25 runs at Hove in the quarter-final of the NatWest Trophy. They batted first and were kept in check by Garth le Roux and Imran Khan, scoring 195 for 9 from their 60 overs. Sussex reached 156 for 4 in reply before Stuart Turner took two wickets in an over, precipitating a collapse to 170 all out.

TUESDAY 5th AUGUST 2003

Nasser Hussain hit an unbeaten 161 from 147 balls as Essex trounced Glamorgan by 145 runs in the National League match at Chelmsford. It was Hussain's highest score in one-day matches, including a six and 21 fours. He and Andy Flower (57) added 176 for the first wicket, and Jonathan Dakin hit 40 from 23 balls to take Essex to 298 for 5. Graham Napier took 4 for 26 when Glamorgan batted as Essex ran out easy winners.

MONDAY 6th AUGUST 1883

Charles Swann was born in Leyton. He played one first-class match for the county, against Yorkshire at Huddersfield in 1912. His debut was delayed as the first day was lost to the weather, and when he finally got to bat on the last day he was part of a spectacular collapse: the last six Essex batsmen (including Swann) all made ducks. It made little difference to the result, as the match was drawn. Swann never played again. He died in Leytonstone in 1960 at the age of 76.

FRIDAY 7th AUGUST 1896

Walter Mead became the first Essex player to take a hat-trick in first-class cricket as the county beat reigning champions Surrey by an innings at Leyton. Surrey struggled on a crumbling pitch as Frederick Bull took 6 for 51 before Mead came on to finish their first innings with two wickets in two balls. Essex led by 201 and enforced the follow-on. Mead came on for the second over of the second innings and bowled the Surrey captain Kingsmill Key with his first ball to complete his hat-trick. He and Bull bowled unchanged and took five wickets each as Surrey were bowled out for 82.

FRIDAY 7th AUGUST 1914

Johnny Douglas and John Freeman put on 261 for the seventh wicket against Lancashire at Leyton, setting a long-standing county record. They came together with the score on 107 for 6, Essex trailing by 72 runs, and batted for four and a half hours. Douglas scored 146 with 15 fours, while Freeman, batting unusually low in the order, hit nine fours in his innings of 106. Essex eventually declared with a lead of over 200, but could not force a victory on the final day.

THURSDAY 7th AUGUST 1947

Peter Smith set a world record when he went in at number 11 against Derbyshire at Chesterfield and proceeded to score 163 in two and a half hours with three sixes and 22 fours. He shared in a county-record last-wicket stand of 218 with Frank Vigar (who finished not out on 114), as Essex rallied from 199 for 9 to reach 417. Smith's achievement was all the more remarkable considering the opposing attack contained three Test bowlers in Cliff Gladwin, Bill Copson, and George Pope. Of course, Smith was actually a highly competent batsman who scored over 1,000 runs that season. But the Essex line-up for this match was unusually strong, with Trevor Bailey and Doug Insole batting at eight and nine respectively. The last-wicket onslaught put Essex into a strong position and they won the match by five wickets.

FRIDAY 7th AUGUST 1959

Essex's match against Gloucestershire at Leyton ended in a tie. Doug Insole scored 177 not out and 90 in the match, and Essex declared on the last day leaving Gloucestershire a target of 212 in just under three hours. This seemed out of reach when they slid to 131 for 8, but a ninth-wicket partnership of 78 between Tony Brown and Barrie Meyer took them to within three runs of victory. Brown dominated the proceedings, hitting four sixes in his 91, but was finally undone by Trevor Bailey when Essex took the new ball. This brought in the last man, Sam Cook. A wide and a single levelled the scores before Barry Knight forced Cook to glove a rising ball and Joe Milner held a diving catch at short leg.

SUNDAY 7th AUGUST 1983

Mark Pettini was born in Brighton. He made his Essex debut in 2001, but his breakthrough season came in 2006, when he scored over 1,200 runs including a career-best 208 not out against Derbyshire at Chelmsford. By the end of the 2011 season he had played 100 first-class matches, scoring 4,907 runs at 32.71 with five centuries. Pettini also made five centuries in one-day matches. He became captain of Essex in 2008 at the age of 24, but resigned in 2010 in order to focus his energies on his batting.

TUESDAY 8th AUGUST 1899

Frederick Fane became the first player to score a double-hundred for the county as Essex reached 673 against Leicestershire at Grace Road. Fane hit 28 fours and a five and shared in big partnerships with Percy Perrin (132) and Charlie McGahey (99). The total was further swelled by career-best scores from Frank Street (76) and George Ayres (83). Essex completed an innings victory the following day.

FRIDAY 9th AUGUST 1929

Essex beat Somerset by two runs in a low-scoring match at Weston-super-Mare. Essex managed only 106 in their first innings, but the spin of Jack O'Connor and Joe Hipkin held Somerset to a lead of 26. Wickets continued to tumble as Essex were dismissed for 103 second time around, leaving Somerset to make just 78 to win. They reached 39 for 2 but Hipkin took 4 for 24 and O'Connor 5 for 34 to bowl them out for 75.

TUESDAY 9th AUGUST 1955

Ray Smith scored the fastest century of the season, hitting 101 not out in 74 minutes against Northamptonshire at Wellingborough. His aggressive hitting made Smith a perennial candidate for this honour, and it was the third time that he achieved the feat. Smith's effort set up a declaration, leaving Northamptonshire to score 332 in 202 minutes — a task they managed for the loss of just three wickets. Their Australian batsman Jock Livingston finished unbeaten on 172, having at one stage threatened to reach his century even more quickly than Smith had done.

SATURDAY 10th AUGUST 1907

Essex beat Sussex by one wicket in a dramatic finish at Leyton. Essex had to chase 236, and made a good start as Frederick Fane scored 86 and Percy Perrin added 42. However, they still needed 23 when the eighth wicket fell. Claude Buckenham — who had earlier taken 11 wickets in the match — held the lower order together with 37. The ninth wicket fell with Essex still needing five to win, but Walter Mead came out to hit the winning boundary.

FRIDAY 10th AUGUST 1984

A century by Graham Gooch helped Essex chase 211 in 33 overs to beat Middlesex at Lord's. Gooch had to contend with indifferent light and a bowling attack that contained Wayne Daniel and the England spin pair Phil Edmonds and John Emburey, but he held the innings together with 105 not out as Essex scored at nearly seven an over and won with seven balls to spare to maintain their challenge for the championship.

MONDAY 11th AUGUST 1924

Joe Hipkin took a hat-trick for Essex in a losing effort against Lancashire at Blackpool. He had Len Hopwood leg-before-wicket and then Dick Tyldesley was caught from the first ball he received. George Duckworth came out to face the hat-trick ball, but rather than offer a dead-bat stroke he advanced out of his crease and was stumped by Frank Gilligan. Hipkin's effort left Essex a target of 210, but they fell to 7 for 3 and eventually lost the match by 35 runs.

THURSDAY 11th AUGUST 1932

Essex were on the receiving end of a second consecutive mauling from Herbert Sutcliffe as they struggled against Yorkshire at Scarborough. Sutcliffe had hit 313 when the sides met at Leyton in June, and he now took the Essex attack apart again with 194 as Yorkshire built a lead of 151. He added 149 with Maurice Leyland in less than an hour, and four overs from Ken Farnes went for 75. The young Farnes was reduced to tears at the close and Essex lost by an innings the following day.

SUNDAY 12th AUGUST 2001

Graham Napier produced a fine all-round performance in Essex's 33-run victory against Worcestershire in the Norwich Union League. Napier arrived at the crease in the first over and hit 73 from 60 balls with four sixes. Essex were bowled out for 200 and Worcestershire reached 122 for 2 in reply before Napier came on to excel with the ball. He took his best one-day figures of 6 for 29 from 7.2 overs as Worcestershire collapsed to 167 all out.

FRIDAY 12th AUGUST 2011

Alastair Cook reached his highest Test score, 294 against India at Edgbaston. He batted for over 11 hours and hit 33 fours, failing by just six runs to become the second Essex batsman to score a triple-century for England. His innings helped England to a mammoth 710 for 7 against a depleted and demoralised Indian attack, and England would win the match by an innings and 242 runs.

WEDNESDAY 13th AUGUST 1997

Essex beat Glamorgan by one wicket in a highly-charged NatWest Trophy semi-final at Chelmsford. The game resumed after being suspended for bad light on the previous evening with Essex — after a late clatter of wickets — still six short of victory with eight wickets down. They added three more runs before Tim Hodgson was caught behind, but last man Peter Such hit the winning runs to take his side to Lord's. The exciting finish was overshadowed by a scuffle that had broken out between Mark Ilott and Robert Croft as the sides left the field on the Tuesday night, for which both players incurred a fine and a suspended ban.

TUESDAY 14th AUGUST 1906

Johnny Douglas took eight wickets to set up an Essex victory against Leicestershire at Southend. It was the first time Essex had played a first-class match away from Leyton, and the county trailed by 23 on first innings. Douglas bowled unchanged through the Leicestershire second innings, taking 8 for 33, with seven of his victims bowled. Leicestershire were all out for 107, and Essex completed a five-wicket victory on the following day.

THURSDAY 14th AUGUST 1980

Essex played in the first major floodlit game of cricket in England. In an experimental match sponsored by the *Daily Mirror*, they beat the touring West Indies at Chelsea's Stamford Bridge ground on a faster scoring rate. The West Indians scored 257 for 9 from 40 overs and Essex replied with 192 for 1 from 28 overs, Graham Gooch (111 not out) and Ken McEwan (65 not out) exploiting the narrow dimensions of the football pitch to great effect.

THURSDAY 15th AUGUST 1901

Essex made their lowest ever total in first-class cricket when they were bowled out by Yorkshire's George Hirst and Wilfred Rhodes for just 30 on a wet wicket at Leyton. They lost their first four wickets for just one run, and only Charlie McGahey (11) and Bill Reeves (10) reached double figures. Essex then dismissed Yorkshire for 104, but by the close they were 15 for 6 in their second innings. They were bowled out the next day for 41 — their fourth-lowest score ever — to lose by an innings. The match was an inauspicious debut for Johnny Douglas, as the future captain made a pair.

WEDNESDAY 15th AUGUST 1951

Left-arm spinner John Childs was born in Plymouth. He had a ten-year career with Gloucestershire before joining Essex in 1985 to replace Ray East. He played 214 first-class matches for the county over the next 12 seasons, taking 604 wickets at an average of 28.06 and scoring 1,153 runs at 10.77. His best season was 1986, when he took 89 wickets at 16.28 to help Essex win the championship. He played two Tests for England against the West Indies in 1988.

SATURDAY 16th AUGUST 1930

Bill Greensmith was born in Middlesbrough. He played 371 first-class matches for the county between 1947 and 1963, taking 720 wickets with his leg-spin at an average of 28.76 and scoring 8,042 runs at 20.10. His only century was an innings of 138 not out against Kent in 1953, while his best bowling performance was 8 for 59 against Gloucestershire in 1956.

WEDNESDAY 16th AUGUST 1978

Having reached the semi-final of the Gillette Cup for the first time, Essex missed out on a Lord's final in a gripping finish against Somerset at Taunton. Essex conceded 287 for 6 as Viv Richards scored a century, but Graham Gooch and Keith Fletcher both scored 50s in reply. However, three batsmen were run out, and Essex reached the last over needing 12 to win. Neil Smith was run out from the last ball attempting to complete a third run that would have won the game. The scores were tied and Essex were eliminated having lost more wickets.

TUESDAY 16th AUGUST 1983

Norbert Phillip finished off Essex's match against Northamptonshire at Wellingborough in grand style by taking a hat-trick. Essex set their opponents a target of 272. The opening pair put on 51, but once John Lever made the breakthrough wickets fell at regular intervals. Phillip had been expensive in his opening spell but came back to dismiss David Steele from the last ball of his ninth over. He then removed Neil Mallender and Jim Griffiths with the first two balls of his tenth over to give Essex a 128-run victory.

SATURDAY 16th AUGUST 2008

Essex won the Friends Provident Trophy, defeating Kent by five wickets in the final at Lord's. They had to chase 215 on a slow pitch and were indebted to a well-paced innings of 70 not out from Grant Flower. Flower shared in partnerships of 68 with James Foster and 57 with Ryan ten Doeschate as Essex won with seven balls to spare. It was the third time that the county had won the season's showpiece one-day final, following NatWest Trophy wins in 1985 and 1997.

TUESDAY 17th AUGUST 1920

George Louden took career-best figures of 8 for 36 to give Essex victory over Derbyshire at Southend. After an evenly contested encounter, Derbyshire needed 202 to win on the last day. However, they found Louden in irresistible form: seven of his victims were clean bowled as the visitors were dismissed for 97 in 32 overs.

MONDAY 17th AUGUST 1953

Seam bowler Jack Bailey marked his Essex debut with 7 for 32 in the second innings against Nottinghamshire at Southend. Essex trailed by 55 after the first innings, but Bailey left them needing only 183 to win. They succumbed to Nottinghamshire's Australian leg-spinner Bruce Dooland and lost by 37 runs. Bailey would go on to play 71 matches for Essex, taking 198 wickets at 22.99. He also captained the Oxford University side in 1958 and served as secretary of MCC from 1974 to 1987.

SATURDAY 18th AUGUST 1928

David Watkins was born in St Albans. He made his debut for Essex in 1949 when he opened the bowling against Northamptonshire. He played a further 11 matches in 1953 and 1954. In all, he took eight wickets at an average of 52.65 and scored 210 runs at 16.15.

WEDNESDAY 19th AUGUST 1981

Essex lost to Derbyshire in the semi-final of the NatWest Trophy at Derby by losing more wickets — the third time in four years that the county had been eliminated from the 60-over competition in this way. Essex struggled to 149 all out on a difficult pitch with Norbert Phillip top-scoring on 42. However, they soon reduced Derbyshire to 30 for 4 and tight bowling from Derek Pringle and Stuart Turner, who between them bowled 24 overs for just 37 runs, kept Essex on top. By the time Phillip began the last over Derbyshire were still ten runs behind, but Paul Newman hit a four from the penultimate ball to reduce the deficit to one. The last ball was pushed back to Phillip, who failed to effect a routine run-out. Derbyshire levelled the scores and advanced to the final.

THURSDAY 20th AUGUST 1846

Thirty years before the foundation of the county club, the first recorded match involving an Essex team took place at the Orsett and Thurrock Club, with Gravesend providing the opposition. The Essex side included Alfred Mynn, probably the leading cricketer of the day, but nevertheless was bowled out for 42 and 39 and lost by eight wickets.

SATURDAY 20th AUGUST 1960

Wicketkeeper Mike Garnham was born in Johannesburg, South Africa. He had been with Gloucestershire and Leicestershire before joining Essex in 1989. He stayed with the county until 1995, appearing in 131 first-class matches, in which he scored 4,157 runs at 29.48 and claimed 267 catches and 18 stumpings. Garnham made four centuries, with a top score of 123 against Leicestershire at Grace Road in 1991. In that match he and Nasser Hussain put on 316 for the fifth wicket to set a county record that stood until 2010.

MONDAY 21st AUGUST 1950

Trevor Bailey took the only hat-trick of his Essex career to finish off the Glamorgan first innings at Newport. He bowled Jim Pleass, then had Norman Hever caught behind, and finally trapped Don Shepherd leg-before-wicket, all with the score on 282. As in Bailey's other landmark bowling achievement — when he had taken all ten wickets against Lancashire a year earlier — Essex lost the match in comprehensive fashion. They were bowled out for 131 and 126 to lose by an innings and 25 runs.

TUESDAY 21st AUGUST 1979

Essex clinched a first County Championship title by beating Northamptonshire while their nearest challengers Worcestershire could only draw at Derby. The title was confirmed with four matches still to play — although it had appeared that the champagne might have to remain on ice for a few more days when Essex were bowled out for 199 on the second day to concede a first-innings lead. Stuart Turner then took 5 for 56 (completing career-best match figures of 10 for 126) to ensure that they had to score only 229 to win. Brian Hardie and Mike Denness put on 113 for the first wicket, and Hardie went on to score an unbeaten century as Essex won by seven wickets. The county won 13 of the 22 matches over the course of the season and would eventually finish with 281 points, 77 clear of Worcestershire. The nucleus of the side had been together for a decade, with Turner, Keith Fletcher, Ray East, John Lever, and David Acfield all having been part of the skeleton staff of 12 players who kept the county afloat in 1969.

SATURDAY 22nd AUGUST 1925

Ken Preston was born in Goodmayes. He played 391 first-class matches for the county between 1948 and 1964, taking 1,155 wickets at an average of 26.22. He initially promised to be an out-and-out fast bowler, but after suffering a broken leg in 1949 he was forced to reduce his pace and rely on movement and accuracy. His finest season was 1957 when he took 140 wickets at 20.35, although his best single-innings figures of 7 for 55 came the previous year against Northamptonshire at Peterborough.

THURSDAY 22nd AUGUST 1946

Denys Wilcox and Reg Taylor added 263 to spark a comeback against Warwickshire at Southend. Essex had closed the first day on 84 for 7 — still 200 runs behind and in danger of following on — but Wilcox hit 134 and Taylor, who was a genuine batsman despite finding himself at number nine, scored 142. The partnership, which remains a county record for the eighth wicket, took Essex into a healthy lead. Ray Smith then took 6 for 41 and the county won by an innings.

TUESDAY 22nd AUGUST 1972

Keith Fletcher scored a brilliant undefeated 139 to lead Essex to victory against Yorkshire at Chelmsford. Essex were chasing a target of 243 in under three hours and soon slumped to 37 for 3. However, Fletcher helped to rebuild the innings in a stand of 114 with Keith Boyce, and then accelerated, hitting four sixes and 12 fours in all. He and Keith Pont added the final 95 runs in a little over seven overs and Essex won by six wickets.

THURSDAY 22nd AUGUST 1974

David Acfield and Stuart Turner put on 122 for the last wicket against Glamorgan at Swansea. The partnership took Essex from 202 for 9, a meagre 14 runs ahead, to 324. Acfield belied his career batting average of 8.18 to score 31 while Turner extended his score from 31 to 118. Essex then reduced Glamorgan to 128 for 5 but were defied on the last day by Alan Jones and his brother Eifion as the Welshmen held out for a draw.

SUNDAY 22nd AUGUST 1982

Ken McEwan scored 156 not out in Essex's John Player League match against Warwickshire at Colchester. Brian Hardie also posted 75 as Essex reached 299 for 4 from their 40 overs. At the time this was the highest total recorded by Essex in the Sunday competition, and yet, incredibly, it was still not enough to win the game. Warwickshire scored 301 for 6 for the victory with three balls remaining.

THURSDAY 22nd AUGUST 1985

Essex beat Hampshire in the semi-final of the NatWest Trophy at Southampton to reach the final of the 60-over competition for the first time. The game went into a second day and resumed with Essex needing 94 from 21.2 overs with six wickets in hand. Significantly, Graham Gooch was still batting, and he scored 93 not out to keep the innings on course. Essex reached the last over one run behind. The first ball was a wide, and Stuart Turner blocked the remaining six deliveries to ensure that Essex won having lost one fewer wicket.

THURSDAY 22nd AUGUST 1996

Ashley Cowan took a hat-trick on the first day against Gloucestershire at Colchester. The hat-trick spanned two overs as the 21-year-old, playing his first full season, dismissed Richard Davis, Martyn Ball, and Andy Smith. Shortly after, he removed Jack Russell to finish with 5 for 68 as Gloucestershire were all out for 280. Essex would go on to build a huge lead, scoring 532 for 8 with Graham Gooch (111), Darren Robinson (72), Paul Prichard (88), and Ronnie Irani (91) all scoring heavily, and they won the match by an innings.

THURSDAY 23rd AUGUST 1917

Ralf Robinson died at Ypres where he was serving as a Second Lieutenant with the Rifle Brigade. He was 32 years old and was one of several Essex cricketers to die in action during the First World War. He was born in Stratford and had kept wicket for Essex in four first-class matches in 1912. He claimed nine catches and four stumpings and scored 25 runs at an average of five.

WEDNESDAY 23rd AUGUST 2000

Essex played their first home floodlit game against Surrey in the National League at Colchester. Nasser Hussain and Stuart Law put on 161 for the first wicket before the innings fell away. The final total of 206 for 8 proved enough, however: no Surrey batsman passed 36, and Essex won by 23 runs. Floodlit cricket would become commonplace across England over the next few years.

THURSDAY 24th AUGUST 1939

Ken Farnes took a hat-trick as Essex defeated Nottinghamshire at Clacton. Essex trailed by 38 after the first innings, but in the second innings Farnes destroyed the heart of the Nottinghamshire batting, accounting for George Heane, Joe Hardstaff, and George Gunn. He finished with 5 for 30 as Nottinghamshire made only 74, and Essex went on to win by seven wickets. Farnes would play only one more match for the county before he died in a wartime plane crash.

WEDNESDAY 24th AUGUST 1949

Trevor Bailey took all ten wickets — only the second time that an Essex bowler had achieved this feat — as Lancashire were bowled out for 331 at Clacton. After the ninth wicket fell, Bailey was given every chance of completing the full set as captain Tom Pearce brought himself on at the other end to bowl gentle medium pace. The last pair of Tattersall and Barlow added 34 before Barlow was bowled by Bailey, who ended with 10 for 90. The batsmen failed to take inspiration from this achievement, however, and were bowled out for 164 and 169 as the county lost by ten wickets.

FRIDAY 25th AUGUST 1905

Johnny Douglas took a hat-trick as Yorkshire were made to follow on at Leyton. Essex had scored 521 and Douglas took wickets with consecutive balls either side of lunch to reduce Yorkshire to 35 for 3. With the last three balls of his next over he bowled Rhodes, Haigh, and Myers to make the score 39 for 6. He finished with 5 for 31 as Yorkshire were dismissed for 98. However, they batted for 150 overs in their second innings to save the match.

TUESDAY 25th AUGUST 1964

Essex beat Australia by six wickets at Southend. The win was built on a first-innings total of 425 for 6, including centuries by Gordon Barker and Keith Fletcher. Essex then dismissed Australia for 218 and 313 in the follow-on, Paddy Phelan taking ten wickets in the match, before knocking off the 107 runs required. It was the county's first victory over Australia since 1905.

TUESDAY 26th AUGUST 1975

Robin Hobbs recorded the fastest century of the season on the last day against Australia at Chelmsford. Set 353 to win, and missing two of their batsmen through injury, Essex were close to defeat when Hobbs went out to bat at 109 for 5 with just John Lever and David Acfield to follow. He proceeded to launch an onslaught against spinners Ashley Mallett and Jim Higgs, hitting 100 out of a partnership of 133 with Brian Hardie. The century took a mere 45 balls and featured 12 fours and seven sixes. The last 50 runs were scored in just 15 balls, including six sixes. However, Hobbs was dismissed immediately after completing his hundred, and the final two wickets followed quickly, leaving Australia winners by 98 runs, and Hardie stranded having carried his bat for 88.

SUNDAY 26th AUGUST 1984

Essex clinched the John Player League title without playing. A victory over Hampshire the previous week had taken them to 46 points, a total that could still be passed by Middlesex and equalled by Nottinghamshire if Essex lost their two remaining matches. But Nottinghamshire lost to Warwickshire and Middlesex lost to Sussex, leaving Essex assured of their second victory in the 40-over competition.

THURSDAY 26th AUGUST 1999

Stuart Law hit a career-best 263 to give Essex a big lead in their match against Somerset. His innings included 36 fours and a six, and he added 275 for the fifth wicket with Darren Robinson (112) as Essex reached 544, nearly 300 runs ahead. Their hopes of victory were dashed on the following day, however, as Somerset held on for a draw with the last pair at the wicket.

THURSDAY 27th AUGUST 1970

Mark Ilott was born in Watford. As a left-arm seam bowler he proved the natural successor to John Lever in the Essex side and played 169 first-class matches between 1988 and 2002, taking 550 wickets at an average of 28.30, with best figures of 9 for 19 against Northamptonshire in 1995. Ilott also scored 2,586 runs at 14.44 with three half-centuries. He was selected for five Tests for England between 1993 and 1995, taking 12 wickets at 45.16.

TUESDAY 27th AUGUST 1974

Graham Gooch scored his maiden first-class century as Essex beat Leicestershire by two wickets at Chelmsford. Leicestershire held the initiative through the first two days of the match and declared at lunchtime on the last day, leaving Essex to make 242 to win. Gooch came in with the score on 73 for 3 and played a commanding innings of 114 not out, including three sixes and eight fours, as Essex won with an over in hand.

TUESDAY 28th AUGUST 1934

Essex opening batsman Dudley Pope reached a century in his last innings for the county. The end-of-season match against his former side Gloucestershire resumed with Pope undefeated on 95, and he duly completed his seventh first-class century before being dismissed for 108. After this the match fizzled out into a draw. Less than two weeks later, Pope suffered fatal injuries when his car collided with a lorry in the village of Writtle.

FRIDAY 28th AUGUST 1953

Essex achieved a fine win over Gloucestershire at Clacton, scoring 311 for 2 in the last innings of the match. The county had trailed by 133 runs after the first innings, but Ken Preston then took 5 for 56 to restrict Gloucestershire to 175. With the pitch now appearing to favour the bowlers, it seemed improbable that Essex would make 309 to win, and their pursuit of victory was further hindered by injuries to Sonny Avery and Doug Insole, who both had to retire hurt. However, Avery, Paul Gibb, and Dick Horsfall all made half-centuries as Essex passed their target with relative ease.

SUNDAY 28th AUGUST 2005

Essex won the ToteSport League with three matches to spare after beating Hampshire at Colchester. Will Jefferson scored 88 from 106 balls as Essex made 222 for 9 from their 45 overs. Hampshire made a good start to their innings and reached 173 for 3, but then lost wickets as they tried to accelerate and finished 12 runs short. Essex lost only one of their 16 league matches and finished 14 points clear of second-placed Middlesex.

MONDAY 29th AUGUST 1938

Ken Farnes took career-best figures of 8 for 38 against Glamorgan at Clacton. Farnes took advantage of a rain-affected pitch and bowled unchanged as Glamorgan were skittled out for 83 in 20.5 overs. He had also taken 7 for 75 in the first innings and finished with match figures of 15 for 113 as Essex won by an innings and 87 runs.

THURSDAY 29th AUGUST 1974

Keith Boyce took a hat-trick as Essex beat Warwickshire by an innings at Chelmsford. Essex had built a first-innings lead of 237 thanks to centuries from Brian Hardie and Bob Cooke. When Warwickshire batted again, Boyce trapped Neil Abberley leg-before-wicket and had Mike Smith caught behind from successive balls. He then had to wait for the start of a new over before he completed his hat-trick by bowling Deryck Murray. That left Warwickshire on 35 for 4, and they were eventually dismissed for 138. Boyce had match figures of 11 for 138 — one of six occasions when he took ten wickets or more in a match for Essex.

FRIDAY 29th AUGUST 1986

Essex beat Somerset from a seemingly impossible position on the last day of the match at Taunton. Somerset required 273 to win and at one stage were 253 for 5 with Ian Botham and Vic Marks both well set. John Childs provided the breakthrough by dismissing Botham for 41, and this sparked a remarkable collapse. The last five wickets fell for ten runs, with Childs and Derek Pringle taking two each. Essex won by nine runs and gained considerable momentum in their challenge for the County Championship.

SATURDAY 30th AUGUST 1890

Harold Palmer was born in Epping. He played 53 first-class matches for the county as an amateur between 1924 and 1932, taking 142 wickets with his leg-breaks at an average of 24.48. He was described by his contemporary Charles Bray as "a tall, thin, awkward-looking player" with an action that was "unorthodox, ugly in fact". However, Bray asserts that he was nevertheless highly effective and might have reached the highest level had he been able to play regularly. He died at Bexhill-on-Sea in Sussex in 1967 at the age of 76.

SATURDAY 30th AUGUST 1902

Playing against Leicestershire at Leyton, Walter Mead, who had gone out to bat as a nightwatchman on the previous evening, batted on for over an hour and extended his score to 119. It was the great bowler's first and only first-class century, and a collection was made to mark the performance, raising £9 13s 1d.

TUESDAY 30th AUGUST 1955

Trevor Bailey and Doug Insole both scored centuries before lunch as Essex declared on 330 for 3 against Nottinghamshire at Southend. The pair added 239 in three hours and both finished unbeaten on 114. It was the last day of the championship season, but Essex failed to end on a winning note as Nottinghamshire successfully chased 311, scoring at over four runs per over and passing their target from the last ball of the match.

SUNDAY 31st AUGUST 1969

Essex ended their first Sunday League season in third place after beating Glamorgan by just one run at Swansea. Essex batted first and scored 180, with Brian Ward making 55. The Glamorgan batsmen took to Ray East, who went for 79 runs from his eight overs, but Keith Boyce and John Lever both bowled superbly, conceding only 20 runs in their combined 16 overs. In the end, Glamorgan fell just short with their last pair at the wicket. Curiously, the championship match that sandwiched this encounter was also decided by a single run, but this time in favour of Glamorgan.

ESSEX CCC
On This Day

SEPTEMBER

THURSDAY 1st SEPTEMBER 1938

Stan Nichols enjoyed the sort of day that usually happens to the hero of a comic strip. He began by extending his overnight score of 123 to 159 as Essex ran up 553, and then followed this up by taking 9 for 37 as Gloucestershire were bowled out for 97. His century included 15 fours and a six, while his bowling stint included a five-over spell of five wickets for six runs. He took a further two wickets before the close as, despite an improved second-innings effort from their opponents, Essex moved towards an easy victory.

TUESDAY 1st SEPTEMBER 1953

Dick Horsfall scored the fastest century of the season to help Essex beat Warwickshire by two wickets at Clacton. Warwickshire set Essex 197 to win at nearly five runs an over, and had them in trouble at 20 for 4, but Horsfall hit a century in 85 minutes. After he was dismissed for 107, Bill Greensmith and Les Savill saw Essex to victory.

THURSDAY 2nd SEPTEMBER 1965

Robin Hobbs took 6 for 30 to help Essex to a two-day victory over Glamorgan at Llanelli. Essex trailed by 72 runs after the first innings, but Hobbs and Barry Knight (4 for 36) bowled the Welsh county out for 113. Hobbs finished with match figures of 12 for 94, and Keith Fletcher scored 72 as Essex won by five wickets. It was only Essex's fourth victory of the season, and they finished just six points above the bottom county.

SUNDAY 2nd SEPTEMBER 1984

Essex beat Derbyshire off the last ball in their John Player League match at Derby. Essex were already assured of the league title, but suffered at the hands of Kim Barnett, whose unbeaten 131 helped Derbyshire to 215. Despite an innings of 64 from Graham Gooch, Essex stuttered to 137 for 6. They were helped by a partnership of 36 between Keith Fletcher and Stuart Turner, but two runs were still needed from the last ball with the last pair at the wicket. Turner hit it for six to win the match in emphatic style.

SUNDAY 3rd SEPTEMBER 1882

Johnny Douglas was born in Clapton. He played 459 first-class matches between 1901 and 1928, scoring 17,915 runs at 28.07 and taking 1,443 wickets at 23.32. In 1914 he was the first player to perform the double of 1,000 runs and 100 wickets in a season for Essex, and he repeated the feat on three further occasions. He held the club captaincy from 1911 until 1928 and gained a reputation as a strict disciplinarian who had little sympathy for anyone whose dedication failed to meet his own phenomenal standards. This commitment was equally prominent in Test cricket, and his dogged approach caused the Australians to suggest that his initials JWHT ought to stand for "Johnny Won't Hit Today". He played 23 Tests, 18 as captain, and led the side when England recovered the Ashes in Australia in 1912. Besides his achievements in cricket, he played amateur football for England and won the gold medal for boxing as a middleweight in the Olympic Games in London in 1908.

MONDAY 3rd SEPTEMBER 1883

John Freeman was born in Lewisham. His uncle Edward was the groundsman at Leyton and played for Essex, while his brother "Tich" Freeman was a notable leg-spin bowler for Kent and England. John played 336 first-class matches for Essex between 1905 and 1928, scoring 14,507 runs at 27.84. He passed 1,000 runs in seven seasons and scored 26 centuries for the county. He often kept wicket and took 229 catches and 47 stumpings. He died in Napsbury, Hertfordshire, in 1958 at the age of 74.

THURSDAY 3rd SEPTEMBER 1992

Essex clinched the County Championship title after defeating Hampshire by eight wickets at Chelmsford. The decisive phase of the match had occurred on the second day when Peter Such and John Childs added 79 for the last wicket to give Essex a lead of 65. Hampshire lost six second-innings wickets before they erased this deficit, but stubborn resistance by the lower order took the match into the fourth day. Essex were set 165 to win, and John Stephenson (83 not out) and Paul Prichard (55 not out) added 133 for the third wicket to guarantee the county a second consecutive title.

FRIDAY 3rd SEPTEMBER 1993

Essex scored 412 in 84 overs to beat Sussex at Hove. The total is the second-highest fourth-innings score ever made by the county, and was achieved for the loss of only three wickets. The match featured high scoring throughout with Sussex making 591 and 312 for 3 while Essex declared their first innings on 493 for 4 with Paul Prichard scoring 225 not out. In their second innings John Stephenson (122) and Nasser Hussain (118) added 215 for the second wicket and Saleem Malik (63) and Graham Gooch (74) finished off the job with an unbeaten stand of 143.

SATURDAY 3rd SEPTEMBER 2005

Twenty-year-old Alastair Cook served notice of his talent with an innings of 214 against Australia at Chelmsford. The tourists had just lost the Ashes series, and Cook added to their discomfort with a dominant performance that included 33 fours and a six. Ravi Bopara also scored 135 and put on 270 with Cook as Essex ran up 502 for 4 from 105 overs on a flat wicket. Australia would respond with 561 for 6 as the two-day match ended in a draw.

TUESDAY 4th SEPTEMBER 1877

Archie Gibson was born in Tadley, Hampshire. He played 23 first-class matches for the county between 1895 and 1910, scoring 492 runs at 14.90, with a highest score of 71 against Kent at Leyton in 1910. Gibson did not play between 1898 and 1909 as he was living first in Russia and then Ceylon (now Sri Lanka), where he was a tea planter. He died in Kenya in 1943 at the age of 65.

SUNDAY 5th SEPTEMBER 1915

Ernest Tedder was born in Woodford Green. He played eight first-class matches in 1946, scoring 208 runs at 14.85. On his debut he made 26 and gave Tom Pearce invaluable support as Essex scored 385 for 8 to beat Somerset, and nine days later he made his best score of 55 against Sussex at Ilford. He ran a hotel in Suffolk and died in Ipswich in 1972 at the age of 67.

SUNDAY 6th SEPTEMBER 1885

George Louden was born in Forest Gate. He played 82 first-class matches for the county between 1912 and 1927, taking 415 wickets at an average of 21.84 and scoring 844 runs at 9.17. When available he made a formidable pace-bowling partnership with Johnny Douglas, but his appearances were limited by ill health and his career as a stockbroker. He took ten wickets in a match on five occasions and had best figures of 8 for 36 against Derbyshire in 1920. He died in Amersham, Buckinghamshire in 1972 at the age of 87.

MONDAY 6th SEPTEMBER 2004

Ronnie Irani hit a limited-overs best 158 not out in the National League against Glamorgan at Chelmsford. Irani batted through all 45 overs of the Essex innings, hitting three sixes and 17 fours. He added 116 for the second wicket with Andy Flower (54) as the total reached 316 for 4. Glamorgan then lost both of their opening batsmen for ducks and were eventually bowled out for 153. The 163-run win ensured Essex's survival in the first division, while Glamorgan had already been confirmed as champions.

SATURDAY 7th SEPTEMBER 1985

Essex won the NatWest Trophy at Lord's, defeating Nottinghamshire in a thrilling final. The foundation of the victory was an opening partnership of 202 between Graham Gooch (91 from 142 balls) and man of the match Brian Hardie, who was run out for 110 from 149 balls. A partnership between Ken McEwan and Derek Pringle then took the final total to a daunting 280 for 2. Despite an opening partnership of 143 by Robinson and Broad, Nottinghamshire always appeared to be losing the game, and came to the last over — to be bowled by Pringle — still needing another 18 runs to win. However, Derek Randall hit fours from the second, fourth and fifth balls to leave just two required from the last ball of the match. It now seemed that the odds were against Essex, with Randall apparently able to score at will, but the last ball was chipped to mid-wicket, where Paul Prichard took the catch to give Essex victory by a single run and secure the county's first NatWest title.

SATURDAY 7th SEPTEMBER 1996

Essex lost the NatWest Trophy final against Lancashire at Lord's despite winning the toss and putting their opponents in to bat. The team batting first had lost the previous ten September finals, as bowlers exploited favourable conditions offered by an early start so late in the year. True to form, Lancashire only managed a modest 186, with Ronnie Irani and Paul Grayson both taking three wickets. However, the Essex innings fell apart against fine bowling from Peter Martin and Glen Chapple. Only three batsmen reached double figures, and Essex were all out for 57 to lose by 129 runs.

SUNDAY 7th SEPTEMBER 1997

Essex won the final of the NatWest Trophy at Lord's, defeating Warwickshire in a match that was put back a day due to the funeral of Princess Diana. After Paul Prichard won the toss, Warwickshire were asked to bat and struggled to 170 with Ashley Cowan taking 3 for 29. Essex had made a mess of chasing a similar target in the previous year's final, but this time there were no such problems: Stuart Law hit 80 not out from 71 balls, including ten fours and a six, and Prichard weighed in with 57 from 45 balls. The target was reached in 26.3 overs for the loss of only one wicket as Essex won the trophy for the second time.

FRIDAY 8th SEPTEMBER 1978

Essex beat Nottinghamshire by nine wickets at Trent Bridge thanks to a century by debutant Alan Lilley. Three declarations were required to produce a result after time had been lost on the first two days. Essex declared 78 behind early on the final day, and were then set a target of 222 in two and a half hours on a pitch that appeared to favour the spinners. However, opening pair Lilley and Gooch made light of this and put on 159 in quick time, with Nottinghamshire's Indian spinner Dilip Doshi — who had taken 4 for 28 in the first innings — proving ineffective. After Gooch fell, the 19-year-old Lilley and Ken McEwan saw Essex to their victory target from just 34.5 overs, with Lilley ending the match unbeaten on exactly 100.

SUNDAY 8th SEPTEMBER 1985

On the day after their epic encounter in the NatWest Trophy final at Lord's, Essex and Nottinghamshire met again in the John Player League at Trent Bridge. Graham Gooch and Brian Hardie, who had shared an opening stand of 202 the previous day, did even better this time, adding 239 for the first wicket, and setting a new record for the competition in the process. Whereas Hardie had outscored Gooch at Lord's, it was now Gooch who led the way, hitting 171 from 135 balls with three sixes and 18 fours, while Hardie made 60. Essex reached 252 for 3 from their 40 overs and won the match in comfort. The win kept them at the top of the league and in position to clinch the trophy on the following Sunday.

TUESDAY 9th SEPTEMBER 1975

Barry Hyam was born in Romford. He played 60 first-class matches for the county as a wicketkeeper between 1993 and 2002, scoring 1,408 runs at 16.76 and taking 167 catches and 13 stumpings. His highest score of 63 came in a losing effort against Glamorgan at Chelmsford in 2001. In 2011 he was appointed the lead wicketkeeping coach for women's and girls' cricket by the England and Wales Cricket Board.

WEDNESDAY 10th SEPTEMBER 1986

Essex clinched their third County Championship title in four seasons during the first day of their match against Nottinghamshire at Trent Bridge. They entered the game needing only three points from their final two fixtures to take the title, and soon began to accumulate bowling points in spite of resistance from Tim Robinson, who made 120. John Lever and Neil Foster shared the first six wickets, but it was Graham Gooch who took the wicket that earned the decisive third bowling point when he had Bruce French caught behind. Essex later added a fourth bowling point as the opposition were dismissed for 267. These would turn out to be the only points Essex would take from the match as they were bowled out for 139 in their first innings and eventually drew the match after some defiant batting on the last day by Keith Fletcher, Alan Lilley, and David East.

THURSDAY 10th SEPTEMBER 1992

Essex scored 442 for 6 in their second innings to beat Derbyshire — the highest fourth-innings score in the county's history. The match had seemed unlikely to provide any records for high scoring when 20 wickets fell on the first day: after bowling out their opponents for 226, Essex were bundled out for 96, with Ian Bishop taking 6 for 18. The pitch played better on the second day as Derbyshire reached 309. Essex then batted for the whole of the third day, recovering from 85 for 3 with the help of John Stephenson (97) and Nadeem Shahid (51). Even so, at the close they were still 167 behind with five wickets left. One of those was that of Graham Gooch, who was batting down the order, and he took control of the match on the last day, scoring an unbeaten 123 and getting support from Mike Garnham (66) and Derek Pringle (28 not out) as Essex completed a historic win.

TUESDAY 11th SEPTEMBER 1984

Essex clinched the County Championship as a result of Somerset's victory over Nottinghamshire on a tense final day of the season. Essex had completed their last match the previous evening, beating Lancashire by ten wickets. This took them to the head of the table, but they would still be overtaken if Nottinghamshire won at Taunton. Nottinghamshire were set 297 to win from 60 overs, and Essex players anxiously followed their progress on the radio. Thirty-six were required from the last three overs and 14 from the last over, with the last pair at the wicket. It still seemed as if the title might slip from Essex's grasp when Mike Bore hit two fours, but he was caught on the boundary attempting the winning hit, and Essex were able to celebrate their third title.

SUNDAY 12th SEPTEMBER 1965

Ian Redpath was born in Basildon. He played seven first-class matches for the county in 1987, scoring 128 runs at 11.63, with a highest score of 46 against Northamptonshire made against part-time bowling at the end of a drawn match. In 1989 he played three matches for Derbyshire, making a pair against Essex in a match at Derby.

SUNDAY 13th SEPTEMBER 1981

Essex won their first John Player League title after beating Surrey at The Oval. They entered the final round of matches with a two-point cushion over Warwickshire, having lost only three matches in the league all year. Essex batted first and were indebted to an innings of 80 not out from Norbert Phillip, including five sixes, as they scored 203 for 7. Phillip hit 34 from the last two overs in an onslaught that put the Essex score out of Surrey's reach. The home side could only manage 182 for 5, and Essex won by 21 runs.

TUESDAY 13th SEPTEMBER 1983

Essex clinched the County Championship by 16 points after bad weather ensured both their game and that of their closest challengers ended in draws. At the start of the last round of matches Essex led Middlesex by 13 points, meaning that they could only be overtaken if they failed to beat Yorkshire and Middlesex beat Nottinghamshire. A washout on the first day at Chelmsford made an Essex victory unlikely, but on day two John Lever took seven wickets and Graham Gooch hit a century to give Essex a lead of 84. On the last day Yorkshire were bowled out for 220, but the rain came before Essex had a chance to knock off the runs. However, the same rain that denied Essex victory also brought Middlesex's match to a premature conclusion, and Essex were crowned champions for the second time.

SATURDAY 13th SEPTEMBER 2008

Essex beat Kent by four wickets to secure promotion from the second division of the NatWest Pro40 League. Both sides harboured hopes of promotion at the outset, and Kent's captain Robert Key gave his side the early initiative with an innings of 120 not out as his side scored 246 for 5 from their 40 overs. Essex lost Mark Pettini to the first ball of their innings, but got back on track with half-centuries from Jason Gallian and Ravi Bopara. However, the crucial innings came from Grant Flower, whose 68 from 42 balls helped Essex win with an over to spare. The victory ensured that Essex remained undefeated in the league and topped their division.

MONDAY 14th SEPTEMBER 1987

Maurice Chambers was born in Port Antonio, Jamaica. He made his first-class debut for Essex against Derbyshire in 2005, but only established himself as a member of the county's pace attack in 2009. By the end of the 2011 season he had played in 34 matches and taken 88 wickets at an average of 32.19. His best performance came against Nottinghamshire at Chelmsford in 2010 when he took 6 for 68 in the first innings and 4 for 55 in the second as Essex beat the eventual champions by 143 runs.

SUNDAY 15th SEPTEMBER 1985

Essex retained their John Player League title, adding the 40-over trophy to the 60-over title they had won a week earlier. The county needed to win their final match, against Yorkshire at Chelmsford, but met resistance from Kevin Sharp who chose this day to hit his best one-day score of 114. Yorkshire posted the challenging total of 231, but 62 from Ken McEwan and 60 from Derek Pringle kept Essex in the game. Paul Prichard hit a quickfire 25 towards the end and Essex won by two wickets with just one ball to spare.

FRIDAY 15th SEPTEMBER 2006

Essex won the inaugural Floodlit Twenty20 Cup competition with a comprehensive win over Derbyshire. The final had been scheduled to be a two-legged affair, but an abandonment at Chelmsford left everything to be decided by the game at Derby. Mark Pettini scored 53 as Essex reached 189 for 7. In reply, Derbyshire collapsed to 38 for 5, and were eventually all out for 97, leaving Essex winners by 92 runs.

FRIDAY 16th SEPTEMBER 1910

Former Essex bowler Frederick Bull was found drowned on the Lancashire coast. He was 35 years old and had left Essex ten years earlier after a career that had seen a meteoric rise and an equally swift decline. Two days before his body was found, he had sent a messenger to his landlady to return his key. He then weighted himself down with stones before entering the sea.

SATURDAY 16th SEPTEMBER 2000

A victory over Warwickshire at Chelmsford gave Essex promotion to the first division of the County Championship after just one season in the new lower tier. Warwickshire also needed a win to have a chance of promotion, and a generous last-day declaration left Essex to score 201 from 56 overs. They fell to 64 for 4 before Ronnie Irani (64 not out) and Stephen Peters (77 not out) took control with a match-winning partnership of 138 from 25 overs.

WEDNESDAY 17th SEPTEMBER 1941

All-rounder Brian Edmeades was born in Matlock, Derbyshire. He played 335 first-class matches for Essex between 1961 and 1976, and unusually his career batting and bowling averages were virtually identical: he scored 12,593 runs at 25.91 and took 374 wickets at 25.90. In his earlier career he was valued more as a medium-pace bowler, but he later became a regular opening batsman. He scored 14 first-class centuries with a top score of 163 against Leicestershire in 1972.

SUNDAY 17th SEPTEMBER 1989

Essex won the Refuge Assurance Cup, an end-of-season play-off competition between the top four Sunday League teams that had been established the previous year. Essex, who had finished third in the league, beat Nottinghamshire in a low-scoring final at Edgbaston by five runs. Paul Prichard top-scored with 57 as they scored 160 for 5 from their 40 overs. Nottinghamshire were bowled out for 155 in reply, with Derek Pringle keeping his cool to take two wickets in the last over of the match.

SUNDAY 17th SEPTEMBER 2006

Essex clinched the NatWest Pro40 title despite losing to Durham by six wickets at Chester-le-Street. Essex recovered from a shaky start to score 201 for 8, with Andy Flower making 81, but Durham put on 152 for the first wicket and passed the Essex total with an over to spare. The defeat meant that Essex could have been overtaken by Sussex, but the Sharks collapsed to defeat against Nottinghamshire at Trent Bridge. This left Essex level on points with Northamptonshire at the top of the table, and they won the title on account of their superior net run rate.

WEDNESDAY 18th SEPTEMBER 1912

Jim Unwin was born in Birdbrook. He served as an officer in the Middlesex Regiment and played seven first-class matches for Essex between 1932 and 1939, scoring 152 runs at 10.85 and failing to take a wicket. However, his main sport was rugby: he played on the wing for Rosslyn Park and England, and toured South Africa with the British Lions in 1938. He died in Perth, Scotland, in 2003 aged 91 and had watched England win the rugby World Cup Final on the previous day.

THURSDAY 18th SEPTEMBER 1958

Derek Pringle was born in Nairobi, Kenya. He played 213 first-class matches for Essex between 1978 and 1993, scoring 6,325 runs at 28.11 with five centuries and taking 566 wickets at 25.37. His all-round skills were especially valuable in one-day cricket, and he was at the forefront of the county's success in that form of the game in the 1980s. He also played 30 Tests for England, averaging 15.10 with the bat and 35.97 with the ball. After retirement he established himself as a leading cricket journalist.

WEDNESDAY 18th SEPTEMBER 1991

Graham Gooch scored 259 as Essex reached 588 for 6 declared in their final match of the season against Middlesex at Chelmsford. He resumed overnight on 202 and advanced to his second-highest score for the county, hitting two sixes and 37 fours, and becoming the first Essex player to pass 250 twice. The innings helped Essex to build a huge first-innings lead and set the stage for them to clinch the County Championship title on the following day.

SATURDAY 18th SEPTEMBER 1999

Essex beat Nottinghamshire despite having been made to follow on after the first innings. They had trailed by 161, but centuries from Paul Prichard and Nasser Hussain allowed them to declare their second innings on 432 for 7, and they bowled Nottinghamshire out for 151 to win by 120 runs. Despite the victory, Essex finished in the lower half of the table, and so found themselves in the second division when the championship was split into two the following year.

WEDNESDAY 19th SEPTEMBER 1990

Jonathan Lewis became the first Essex player to score a century in his maiden first-class innings in the end-of-season match against Surrey at The Oval. The 20-year-old was given a debut as several established players were unavailable, and he came in at number seven towards the end of the first day with the score on 275 for 5. He was 25 not out overnight, and on the second day took his score to 116 with 15 fours before he ran out of partners. By that time the Essex score had reached 539. Middlesex had to follow on but scored 613 for 6 in their second innings to save the game.

THURSDAY 19th SEPTEMBER 1991

Essex clinched the County Championship by completing a comfortable innings victory over Middlesex at Chelmsford. Essex needed to win their final match of the season to hold off the challenge of Warwickshire, and began in spectacular fashion by bowling out the visitors for a paltry 51, Middlesex's lowest ever total against Essex. The Essex batting was in complete contrast: they scored 566 for 6, the county's highest ever score against Middlesex, with Graham Gooch making 259. Middlesex trailed by a small matter of 515 runs, but produced a better batting performance in their second innings and reached 307. Essex finally secured the title shortly after lunch on the third day when Neil Foster had Dean Headley caught in the gully by Saleem Malik. The celebrations were all the sweeter as Essex had been runners-up for the previous two seasons.

WEDNESDAY 20th SEPTEMBER 1893

Frank Gilligan was born in the Denmark Hill district of London. He did not quite match the success of his younger brothers Arthur and Harold, who both captained England, but he kept wicket for Essex in 78 first-class matches between 1919 and 1929, scoring 1,808 runs at an average of 22.32 and claiming 87 catches and 34 stumpings. Gilligan's availability was restricted because of his job as a schoolteacher, and in 1930 he emigrated to New Zealand to take up a headmastership, later winning the OBE for his services to education. He died in Wanganui in 1960 at the age of 66.

WEDNESDAY 20th SEPTEMBER 1916

Henry Keigwin died in action near Thiepval in the Somme aged 35. He had played four first-class matches for Essex in 1906 and 1907, scoring 69 runs at an average of 11.50 and taking four wickets at 44.75, but his involvement with the county finished after he moved to Scotland to become director of music at Trinity College, Glenalmond.

SATURDAY 21st SEPTEMBER 2002

Essex chased an imposing target of 340 to beat Nottinghamshire at Chelmsford and clinch the County Championship second division title. The county faced a 59-run deficit after the first innings, but bowled out the visitors for 280. Will Jefferson then played a fine innings of 165 not out to steer Essex to victory. He hit 29 fours and shared in partnerships of 135 for the third wicket with Mark Waugh (76) and an unbeaten 138 for the fourth wicket with Aftab Habib (57 not out). This was Essex's fifth consecutive win in the championship and marked the end of a triumphant first season as coach for Graham Gooch.

WEDNESDAY 22nd SEPTEMBER 1976

Seam bowler Ricky Anderson was born in Hammersmith. He played 32 first-class matches for the county between 1999 and 2001, taking 109 wickets at an average of 24.77 with best figures of 6 for 34 against Northamptonshire in 2000. He also scored 471 runs at an average of 13.85. After leaving Essex he appeared in eight matches for Northamptonshire and played Minor Counties cricket for Cambridgeshire.

FRIDAY 23rd SEPTEMBER 2011

Ravi Bopara set a record for the best bowling analysis for England in international Twenty20 matches when he took 4 for 10 against the West Indies at The Oval. His medium-pace bowling came into its own on a pitch that offered little help to the faster bowlers, and he maintained an accurate line and length to dismiss Nkruma Bonner, Christopher Barnwell, Danza Hyatt, and Darren Sammy in the space of 15 balls. The West Indies were all out for 125, and England romped to a ten-wicket victory — the first time they had achieved this margin in Twenty20 internationals.

FRIDAY 24th SEPTEMBER 1971

Pace bowler Darren Cousins was born in Cambridge. He played 15 first-class matches for Essex between 1993 and 1998, taking 27 wickets at an average of 42.14 with best figures of 6 for 35 against Cambridge University in 1994. He also played in 46 one-day matches, taking 52 wickets at 28.90. After leaving Essex, he played briefly for Surrey and then spent three seasons with Northamptonshire.

THURSDAY 24th SEPTEMBER 2009

Danish Kaneria took a hat-trick against Derbyshire to help Essex's cause as they sought to gain promotion to the first division of the County Championship. Derbyshire were looking to post a huge total when they finished the first day on 368 for 3, but the Pakistani Test bowler helped to bring Essex back into the match on the second day by bowling Greg Smith and having Graeme Wagg and Jonathan Clare leg-before-wicket. These were Kaneria's only wickets of the innings, but they helped to restrict Derbyshire to 474 all out.

SUNDAY 25th SEPTEMBER 2005

Essex defeated Northamptonshire by seven wickets in their final National League match of the season at Northampton. The home side were bowled out for 208 with three balls of the 45 overs remaining. Essex then lost openers Will Jefferson and Ronnie Irani cheaply, but the innings was turned around by a third-wicket stand of 168 between Alastair Cook (94 with 16 fours) and Grant Flower (88 not out with nine fours). This partnership set Essex up to win the match with more than four overs in hand. The victory completed a triumphant campaign in which Essex lost only once and finished 14 points clear at the top of the league table.

SUNDAY 26th SEPTEMBER 1915

Essex all-rounder Geoffrey Davies was killed in action at Hulluch in France while serving on the Western Front as a captain in the Essex Regiment. He was 22 years old. The previous year, in his final first-class match, he had taken 4 for 18 and scored 118 against Somerset, giving notice of a huge promise that was never to be fulfilled.

SUNDAY 26th SEPTEMBER 1937

Colin Hilton was born in Atherton, Lancashire. He was a genuinely fast bowler who began his career with his native county but joined Essex for the 1964 season. That year he played 24 first-class matches, taking 58 wickets at an average of 34.46. Unfortunately, his arrival at Essex coincided with a change in the no-ball rule, and he had difficulty adjusting to the new regulation which required him to keep his front foot behind the popping crease. Disillusioned with being called frequently for overstepping, he turned his back on county cricket at the end of the season at the age of 26.

THURSDAY 26th SEPTEMBER 1957

Matthew Fosh was born in Epping. He played 14 first-class matches for the county between 1976 and 1978, scoring 481 runs at an average of 20.91, with a top score of 66 against Kent at Folkestone in 1977. Much was expected of him after a promising career at Harrow School and Cambridge University, but he dropped out of cricket and had a successful career in business management. Interviewed by the *Daily Telegraph* in 2006, he recalled how he felt differently about the game than players such as Mike Gatting and David Gower, with whom he played for England Young Cricketers: "They seemed to have an application and desire for the game that I as a dyed-in-the-wool Corinthian amateur lacked. There were too many other things that I wanted to try."

SATURDAY 26th SEPTEMBER 2009

Essex gained promotion from the second division of the County Championship after beating Derbyshire by five wickets. Essex conceded a first-innings lead of 118, but picked up enough bonus points to ensure that they would still oust Northamptonshire for a promotion spot if they won. A declaration by Derbyshire on the final day left them to make 359 from 65 overs, and they looked like second favourites when Ryan ten Doeschate joined Mark Pettini with the score at 203 for 5. However, the pair added the remaining 156 runs in 17.3 overs, with ten Doeschate hitting a brilliant 108 from only 59 balls, including eight sixes and nine fours. Pettini finished on 85 from 94 balls, his second year as captain ending with a thrilling success.

MONDAY 27th SEPTEMBER 1926

Ernest Stanley was born in Leyton. He played 13 first-class matches for the county between 1950 and 1952, scoring 226 runs at 12.55, with a highest score of 35 against Yorkshire at Bradford in 1951. He was also a useful footballer who played for Arsenal.

TUESDAY 28th SEPTEMBER 1886

Harry Hills was born in Mayland. He was a leg-break bowler who played 14 first-class matches for the county between 1912 and 1919, taking 15 wickets at 49.20 and scoring 139 runs at 8.17. On his debut he took 5 for 63 as Essex made the Australians follow on, but he was never to match those figures again.

TUESDAY 29th SEPTEMBER 2009

Ravi Bopara scored 30 in a losing cause as England were defeated by New Zealand in the Champions Trophy at Johannesburg. Bopara came in with the score at 50 for 4 and stayed for 16 overs in testing conditions as he tried to see England to a defensible score. He hit only two fours and was eventually trapped leg-before-wicket by a shooter from Shane Bond. England's total of 146 proved too little, but both countries qualified for the semi-finals of the tournament.

MONDAY 30th SEPTEMBER 1872

Edward Sewell was born in Lingsugur, India, where his father was stationed in the British Army. He was educated in England, but then returned to India to work as a civil servant and scored heavily in Indian cricket. He moved back to England at the start of the 20th century and played 55 matches for Essex between 1902 and 1904, scoring 1,822 runs at 21.18 with two centuries. He was also a fine rugby player, and after retiring as a player he wrote several books about both sports.

ESSEX CCC
On This Day

OCTOBER

WEDNESDAY 1st OCTOBER 1890

Oswell Borradaile was appointed club secretary. He would hold the post for over 30 years, and play a large part in keeping the club afloat during a period when it struggled to attract members and raise funds. Like many of the club's administrators in its early years, he also played for the county, although his first-class career amounted to a single match against Surrey in 1894, when he scored two and five. He died in Bexhill-on-Sea, Sussex, in 1935 at the age of 76.

MONDAY 1st OCTOBER 1917

Norman Borrett was born in Wanstead. He played three first-class matches for the county on either side of the Second World War, scoring 33 runs at 16.50. He later played Minor Counties cricket for Devon. However, his cricketing achievements pale into insignificance when compared with his feats in other sports: Borrett was an international squash player who won the British Amateur Championship five times; and he also captained the Great Britain hockey team to an Olympic silver medal at the 1948 games in London.

MONDAY 2nd OCTOBER 1972

Syd Puddefoot died in Rochford at the age of 77. He played eight first-class matches for the county in 1922 and 1923, scoring 101 runs at an average of 16.83, but was better known in his day as a footballer. Puddefoot played for West Ham United, Falkirk, and Blackburn Rovers, picking up five caps for England and scoring a goal in the 1928 FA Cup Final. His transfer from West Ham to Falkirk for £5,000 constituted a world record at the time. He later had a career in football management, coaching in Turkey and becoming manager of Northampton Town in the years before the Second World War.

SATURDAY 3rd OCTOBER 1891

Michael Green was born in Bristol. He had played 91 first-class matches for Gloucestershire before he played in two games for Essex in 1930. He scored just 27 runs for the county at an average of 6.75. Green later served as secretary of Worcestershire and managed the England touring team to Australia in 1950/51.

THURSDAY 4th OCTOBER 1990

Frederick St George Unwin died in Braintree aged 79. He was born in Halstead and played 53 first-class matches as an amateur for the county between 1932 and 1950, scoring 1,138 runs at 14.58. Unwin was part of a three-headed captaincy team (along with JWA Stephenson and Denys Wilcox) for the 1939 season to fill the vacancy caused by Tom Pearce's unavailability. Despite this lack of continuity, Essex finished fourth in the championship, their best showing for more than 40 years.

SATURDAY 5th OCTOBER 1963

Andrew Golding was born in Colchester. He was a slow left-arm bowler who played only one first-class match for the county, against New Zealand in 1983. He bowled Ian Smith in both innings, and was not dismissed in the match, scoring two not out and six not out. He later played for Cambridge University, Suffolk, and Northumberland.

THURSDAY 5th OCTOBER 2000

Nasser Hussain scored 95, his second-highest score in one-day internationals, to lead England to victory over Bangladesh in the preliminary round of the ICC Trophy in Nairobi. An upset was not entirely out of the question when Bangladesh scored 232 for 8 from their 50 overs, but Hussain hit five sixes and nine fours and shared a second-wicket partnership of 175 with Alec Stewart as England won with more than six overs to spare. Any pleasure in the victory was short-lived, however, as his side would fall to South Africa in the next round.

SATURDAY 6th OCTOBER 1900

One of the county's greatest players, Maurice "Stan" Nichols, was born in Stondon Massey. He played 418 first-class matches between 1924 and 1939, scoring 15,736 runs at 26.31 and taking 1,608 wickets (the second most by an Essex bowler) at an average of 21.26. He achieved the double of 1,000 runs and 100 wickets in a season for Essex no fewer than eight times — no other Essex player has managed it more than four. During the 1930s Nichols was probably the premier all-rounder in the country and he played 14 Tests for England.

FRIDAY 7th OCTOBER 1887

Charles Albert George Russell, better known as "Jack", was born in Leyton. He was the county's leading batsman in the first quarter of the 20th century, playing 379 first-class matches and scoring 23,610 runs at an average of 40.91, including 62 centuries. He passed 1,000 runs in a season 13 times despite losing four seasons to the First World War. Russell was also a useful medium-pace bowler and took 276 wickets for the county at 27.10. He was unlucky to play only ten Tests, but in these he managed three centuries and had an average of 56.87.

FRIDAY 7th OCTOBER 1983

Dwayne Bravo was born in Santa Cruz, Trinidad. A former West Indian captain, and one of the leading all-rounders in world cricket, he made only one appearance for Essex, recruited for the finals day of the Friends Provident Twenty20 in 2010 and flown in from the Caribbean in the hope he would help the county win the trophy. The move failed to pay dividends: in the semi-final against Hampshire, he was run out for five and then bowled four overs that cost 46 runs — with 17 taken from his last over, the penultimate one of the innings — as Essex were defeated by six wickets.

SATURDAY 8th OCTOBER 1994

Former Essex star Saleem Malik finished the day unbeaten on 155 as Pakistan fought to save the second Test against Australia after following on in Rawalpindi. He would go on to reach a career-best 237 as the match petered out into a tame draw and all of Australia's players had a turn at bowling with the exception of wicketkeeper Ian Healy.

SATURDAY 9th OCTOBER 1943

Robert Hyndson died in Bradford. He was born in Cape Town, South Africa, in 1894, and played a single first-class match for Essex against the Australian Imperial Forces in 1919. His scores of six and one failed to impress, and when he bowled he conceded 71 runs without taking a wicket. Essex lost the match by 309 runs, and Hyndson never appeared again.

FRIDAY 10th OCTOBER 2008

Stan Cray died in Torquay, Devon, aged 87. He played in 99 first-class matches for the county between 1938 and 1950, scoring 4,062 runs at an average of 24.46. His most successful season was 1947, when he scored 1,339 runs including three centuries. After being released by Essex, Cray served as a club professional for Paignton and played Minor Counties cricket for Devon.

MONDAY 11th OCTOBER 1943

Keith Boyce was born in the parish of St Peter on the island of Barbados. He ranks as one of the most exciting players to have played for the county, noted for his fast bowling, powerful hitting, and athletic fielding. His talent was spotted by Trevor Bailey during a tour of the West Indies as a member of the Rothman Cavaliers and he was brought to Essex to gain residential qualification. Boyce played 211 first-class matches for the county between 1966 and 1977, scoring 6,848 runs at 22.75 and taking 662 wickets at 23.72. He also played 21 Tests for the West Indies and was a member of their victorious team in the inaugural World Cup in 1975. He died in Barbados on his 53rd birthday in 1996.

FRIDAY 12th OCTOBER 1906

Ivan Chapman was born in Pudsey, Yorkshire. He played only one first-class match for Essex, a draw against Middlesex at Leyton in 1929, in which he scored nine runs in his only innings and did not take a wicket in seven overs. He died in Waikato, New Zealand, in 1976.

THURSDAY 13th OCTOBER 1892

Slow left-arm bowler Harry Mortlock was born in Hackney. He played three first-class matches for Essex in 1912, taking five for 104 in the second innings of his debut match to seal an innings victory over Derbyshire. However, he took only two wickets in his other two games. In the First World War he served as a captain in the London Regiment, and after the war he played in one further match — some nine years after his previous appearance — but failed to make an impact in a drawn game against Lancashire at Leyton.

THURSDAY 14th OCTOBER 1993

West Indian spin bowler Carlos "Bertie"Clarke died in Putney aged 75. He was born in Barbados and played three Tests for the West Indies against England in 1939, after which he remained in London and qualified as a doctor. After the war he played for Northamptonshire for four years and took the final wicket in a tie against Essex in 1947. He was already 41 when he made his Essex debut, but played 18 matches for the county in 1959 and 1960, taking 58 wickets at a highly respectable average of 23.32, with a best performance of 7 for 130 against his former county Northamptonshire in 1959. In the 1960s Clarke was convicted of performing illegal abortions and served time in prison. However, he was later recognised for his work with young people in London's Caribbean community and received the OBE in 1983.

TUESDAY 15th OCTOBER 1895

Hugh Wagstaff was born in Romford. He played five first-class matches for Essex in 1920 and 1921, scoring 19 runs at 9.50 and taking two wickets at an average of over 60. He died in Hornchurch in 1970.

SATURDAY 16th OCTOBER 1880

Edward John Freeman was born in Lewisham into a cricketing family. His father, Edward Charles Freeman, was the groundsman at Leyton and played for Essex from 1887 to 1896, and his cousins John Freeman, Tom Russell, and Jack Russell all became notable figures in Essex cricket. He never quite reached their heights, but nevertheless played in 55 first-class matches between 1904 and 1912, scoring 1,280 runs at 14.54 with seven half-centuries.

THURSDAY 17th OCTOBER 1889

A special general meeting was held in London's Great Eastern Hotel to discuss the club's precarious financial position. The club was running a large deficit and was having difficulty satisfying its bankers, and there was a stark warning from the chair that it was in danger of being wound up. An appeal raised sufficient funds to keep the club afloat, but financial pressures would continue to dog Essex cricket for many years to come.

TUESDAY 17th OCTOBER 1967

Seam bowler Alastair Fraser was born in Edgware, Middlesex. He followed his older brother Angus Fraser into the Middlesex team but managed only a handful of games and moved to Essex in 1991. He scored an unbeaten 52 in his first match, against Sussex at Horsham, but managed only three wickets in five first-class matches over two years, and later rejoined Middlesex.

FRIDAY 18th OCTOBER 1968

Stuart Law was born in Brisbane, Australia. He joined Essex as an overseas player in 1996 and played 92 first-class matches for the county, scoring 8,538 runs at an average of 58.88 including 30 centuries. He also scored 11 centuries and 15 half-centuries in his 121 one-day matches, and was a key member of the side that won the NatWest Trophy in 1997 and the Benson and Hedges Cup the following year. Law was named as one of *Wisden's* Cricketers of the Year in 1998 and was the Professional Cricketers' Association Player of the Year for 1999. He left Essex after the 2001 season to join Lancashire.

MONDAY 19th OCTOBER 1953

Steve Malone was born in Chelmsford. He played only two first-class matches for Essex in 1975 and 1978 — both against Cambridge University — and took two wickets against the students at an average of 50.50. He failed to establish himself in the first team at Essex and later moved on to play for Hampshire, Glamorgan, and Durham.

MONDAY 20th OCTOBER 1941

Essex and England fast bowler Ken Farnes died at the age of 30 when the Wellington Bomber he was flying crashed on a night flight over the Midlands. He had joined the Royal Air Force Volunteer Reserve in the previous year and had recently returned to Britain after training as a pilot in Canada. Farnes stands alongside Hedley Verity as one of the great losses that English cricket suffered during the Second World War. After the war a scoreboard was set up at the Gidea Park ground in Romford in his memory, with a plaque bearing the inscription: "His spirit shall endure".

MONDAY 21st OCTOBER 1889

Brian Castor was born in Demerara, Guyana. He was appointed as the club's first permanent secretary in 1930 and held the post until 1946, later holding a similar position at Surrey. He was also a useful player, having represented Middlesex Colts as a young man. Castor captained Essex against Cambridge University in 1932, and scored 13 in his only innings. After the retirement of Whiz Morris at the end of the 1932 season, Castor was considered as a possible successor as county captain, although he was 43 and his first-class experience amounted to that one match against Cambridge, but other counties raised objections to the proposed arrangement. His service to the club was interrupted by the Second World War, when he served with the army in Singapore and survived a three-year ordeal as a prisoner-of-war.

THURSDAY 22nd OCTOBER 1914

David Cock was born in Great Dunmow. He was a farmer who played 14 first-class matches for the county in 1939 and 1946, scoring 355 runs at 19.72 and also keeping wicket. His highest score was 98 which set up an innings victory over Somerset at Westcliff-on-Sea in 1939. Cock also played Minor Counties cricket for Hertfordshire and Cambridgeshire.

SUNDAY 22nd OCTOBER 1978

Owais Shah was born in Karachi, Pakistan. He joined Essex in 2010 after a lengthy career with Middlesex, during which he established himself as a high-quality batsman and played six Tests, 71 one-day internationals, and 17 Twenty20 matches for England. Shah had also played in South Africa for the Cape Cobras and in New Zealand for Wellington, as well as for the Kolkata Knight Riders in the Indian Premier League. He played ten first-class matches for Essex in 2011, scoring 574 runs at 33.76, including centuries against Leicestershire and Glamorgan.

SATURDAY 23rd OCTOBER 1897

Gerald Ridley was born in Felsted, where his family owned one of Essex's leading breweries. He played six first-class matches for the county between 1922 and 1926, scoring 113 runs at 10.27, with a top score of 54 against Gloucestershire at Colchester in 1924.

THE TALLEST PLAYER TO REPRESENT ESSEX WILL JEFFERSON WAS BORN IN OCTOBER 1979 – SEE OVER

TUESDAY 24th OCTOBER 2000

Nasser Hussain scored 73 to help England chase down 305 in the first one-day international against Pakistan in Karachi. He came out to bat in the first over after Alec Stewart was controversially given out, and scored his runs from 99 balls with eight fours, putting on 114 for the third wicket with Graeme Hick. After Hussain was dismissed, Graham Thorpe and Andrew Flintoff saw England to a five-wicket victory. England lost the other two one-dayers, but the tour would end on a triumphant note for Hussain as he led England to a 1-0 win in the Test series.

THURSDAY 25th OCTOBER 1979

Will Jefferson was born in Derby. At 6 feet and 9½ inches, he is the tallest player to have represented Essex. He made his debut in 2000 and played in 61 first-class matches for the county, scoring 4,136 runs at an average of 41.77, including 11 centuries. Jefferson's match-winning 165 not out against Nottinghamshire secured the County Championship second division title in 2002, but his finest season for the county was 2004, when he averaged 55.53 and scored a career-best 222 against Hampshire at the Rose Bowl. He moved to Nottinghamshire after the 2006 season, and later played for Leicestershire.

THURSDAY 25th OCTOBER 1995

Alan Lavers died in Aberdeen, Scotland, at the age of 83. He was born in Melbourne, Australia, but was educated at Chigwell School and played 25 matches for Essex as an amateur between 1937 and 1953, scoring 695 runs at 16.54 and taking 13 wickets with his off-breaks at an average of 37.15.

WEDNESDAY 26th OCTOBER 1892

Geoffrey Davies was born in Poplar. He played 32 matches for Essex as an all-rounder between 1912 and 1914, scoring 757 runs at 17.60, including two centuries, and taking 68 wickets at an average of 26.01. He also played for Cambridge University in 1913 and 1914, which restricted his availability for the county side. His career was cut short by the First World War, and he was killed in action in 1915 at the age of just 22.

TUESDAY 26th OCTOBER 1971

All-rounder and former Essex captain Ronnie Irani was born in Leigh, Lancashire. He joined Essex from Lancashire in 1994 and played 211 first-class matches for the county, scoring 12,944 runs at 43.43 and taking 316 wickets at an average of 29.24. After 2004 a knee injury prevented him from bowling, but he was still more than worth his place in the side as a batsman. He captained Essex for eight seasons from 2000 until retirement in 2007, winning the ToteSport National League title in 2005 and its successor the NatWest Pro40 in 2006. Irani also played three Tests and 31 one-day internationals for England without ever winning a regular place.

SUNDAY 27th OCTOBER 1918

Eric Price was born in Middleton, Lancashire. He was a slow left-arm bowler who played two seasons for his native county immediately after the Second World War. He then played 43 first-class matches for Essex in 1948 and 1949, taking 92 wickets at an average of 32.75. Price was one of the chief victims when Australia scored 721 in a day at Southend in 1948, bowling 20 overs at a cost of 156 runs without taking a wicket. But he also had his good days, with a best performance of 8 for 125 against Worcestershire in 1949.

SUNDAY 28th OCTOBER 1906

Dudley Pope was born in Barnes, Surrey. He started his career with Gloucestershire before playing 148 first-class matches for Essex between 1928 and 1934, scoring 6,443 runs at an average of 27.53, including seven centuries. He had just completed his most prolific season when he died in a car crash in September 1934 at the age of 27.

SUNDAY 28th OCTOBER 1917

Former Essex cricketer James Valiant died in Palestine where he was serving as a Lieutenant in the Royal Welsh Fusiliers. He was 33 years old. Valiant played in one first-class match for Essex, against Northamptonshire in 1912, and bowled four overs without taking a wicket. Essex were out for 60 and 81 to lose by an innings inside two days, with Valiant's contribution an unbeaten nought followed by three.

SUNDAY 29th OCTOBER 1939

Roger Wrightson was born in Elsecar, Yorkshire. He was a left-handed batsman who played 12 first-class matches for Essex between 1965 and 1967, scoring 332 runs at an average of 20.75. His best performance came against Warwickshire at Clacton in 1965 when he came in with the score at 7 for 4 and scored 84 to take Essex to a narrow first-innings lead in a match they would ultimately draw. Wrightson quit first-class cricket to pursue a career in teaching, although he later played some Minor Counties cricket for Cumberland. He died in Carlisle in 1986 at the age of 46.

FRIDAY 30th OCTOBER 1908

Essex's leading all-time wicket-taker, Peter Smith, was born in Ipswich. He played 434 first-class matches for the county between 1929 and 1951, taking 1,610 wickets with his leg-breaks and googlies at an average of 26.28, and capturing ten wickets in a match on no fewer than 27 occasions. He was also an able batsman who made 9,652 runs at 18.14, including eight centuries. Smith's finest season was 1947 when he achieved the double of 1,000 runs and 100 wickets and was named one of *Wisden's* Cricketers of the Year. His haul of 172 wickets in that season remains an Essex record, while his score of 163 against Derbyshire is a world record for a number 11 batsman.

THURSDAY 31st OCTOBER 1912

Nicholas Vere-Hodge was born in Woodford Green. He played 23 first-class matches for Essex between 1936 and 1939, scoring 713 runs at an average of 22.28, including two centuries. Vere-Hodge had a successful career in medicine and became a Fellow of the Royal College of Surgeons. He died in Salisbury, Wiltshire, in 2005 at the age of 93.

ESSEX CCC
On This Day

NOVEMBER

WEDNESDAY 1st NOVEMBER 1989

Future Essex player Saleem Malik helped to guide Pakistan to victory in the final of the Nehru Trophy against West Indies at Calcutta (now Kolkata). Two days after his quickfire 66 had seen off England in the semi-final, he struck 71 from 62 balls with six fours and a six against a strong West Indian attack. He was dismissed with Pakistan still 48 short of their target, but Imran Khan and Wasim Akram saw them home by four wickets to win the six-nation tournament.

FRIDAY 2nd NOVEMBER 1934

Sid Hadden died in Whipps Cross at the age of 57. He was a wicketkeeper who played four first-class matches for Essex in August 1912 and a further two in July 1920, taking five catches and making one stumping. He batted in the lower order and scored 29 runs at 9.66.

FRIDAY 3rd NOVEMBER 1905

Tom Pearce was born in Stoke Newington. He played 231 first-class matches between 1929 and 1950, scoring 11,139 runs at 33.96, including 20 centuries. He played as an amateur, but his employer was a former Essex player and a keen supporter of the club so Pearce was allowed generous opportunities to play. He was able to assume a share of the captaincy from 1933 to 1938, and after the war he became sole captain, handing over to Doug Insole in 1950. After he retired as a player he served as the club's chairman and president. Pearce was also at various times a Test selector and MCC tour manager, and was awarded the OBE in 1979 for his services to cricket. He died in Worthing in 1994 at the age of 88.

FRIDAY 4th NOVEMBER 1994

Saleem Malik began a successful rearguard action as Pakistan fought to save the final Test against Australia at Lahore. Facing a first-innings deficit of 82, he came in with the score on 28 for 2 and remained unbeaten on 59 at the close of play. The following day he would go on to make 143 as his side secured the draw and a 1-0 series win.

THURSDAY 5th NOVEMBER 1987

Graham Gooch made a brilliant century to take England to the World Cup Final. His side were considered heavy underdogs in the semi-final against hosts India at Bombay (now Mumbai), but Gooch scored 115 from 136 balls with 11 fours on a turning pitch as England put up a score of 254. His innings was based around a pre-match plan of using the sweep shot against the Indian spinners Ravi Shastri and Maninder Singh, and he was supported by Mike Gatting in a key partnership of 117 for the third wicket. When India batted, Gooch's Essex team-mate Neil Foster removed three top-order batsmen and England ran out winners by 35 runs.

SATURDAY 6th NOVEMBER 1897

Jack O'Connor was born in Cambridge. He played 516 first-class matches for the county between 1920 and 1939, scoring 27,722 runs at 35.18 and taking 537 wickets at an average of 32.63. He scored over 1,000 runs in a season 16 times, and four times passed 2,000 runs, with a highest aggregate of 2,308 (made at an average of 56.29) in 1934. O'Connor hit 71 centuries for the county — more than any other player apart from Graham Gooch — with a highest score of 248 against Surrey at Brentwood in 1934. He also played in four Tests for England. He died at Buckhurst Hill in 1977.

THURSDAY 7th NOVEMBER 1901

Max Raison was born in Wanstead. He played 17 first-class matches for the county as an amateur between 1928 and 1930, scoring 451 runs at 18.04 and taking 14 wickets at an average of 41.07. His main career was in publishing: he was managing editor of *Picture Post* and later a founder and managing director of *New Scientist*. He died in Theberton, Suffolk, in 1988 at the age of 86.

SUNDAY 8th NOVEMBER 1981

Andrew McGarry was born in Basildon. He played 19 first-class matches for the county between 1999 and 2007, taking 29 wickets at an average of 53.31. His best performance came when he took 5 for 27 against Cambridge University in 2003.

SUNDAY 8th NOVEMBER 1987

Graham Gooch and Neil Foster played for England in the World Cup Final against Australia at Calcutta (now Kolkata), but it was another Essex player, Australian captain Allan Border, who would end up on the winning side. Gooch failed to repeat his semi-final heroics and fell for 35, while Border — not usually known as a bowler — chipped in with two key wickets as England fell seven short of Australia's score.

SUNDAY 9th NOVEMBER 1975

Andrew Clarke was born in Brentwood. He played ten first-class matches for the county between 2002 and 2004, scoring 179 runs at 14.91 and taking 26 wickets at an average of 29.30. His finest performance came in a National League 45-over match against Yorkshire in 2003, when he took 4 for 28 to help Essex to a four-wicket victory.

SUNDAY 10th NOVEMBER 1872

Harold Arkwright was born in Oswestry, Shropshire. He was an Old Etonian who played three first-class matches for Essex in 1894 and 1895 while on vacation from Oxford University, taking four wickets at an average of 27.25. Arkwright was later a director of Barclay's Bank.

TUESDAY 10th NOVEMBER 1903

A special general meeting was held to discuss the club's financial deficit, which had increased as a result of falling membership and bad weather the previous year. The situation was exacerbated by the demands of Essex's leading professional, Walter Mead, for an increase in the pay he received during the off-season. The club could not agree to Mead's demands, and the great bowler would not appear for Essex again until 1906.

TUESDAY 10th NOVEMBER 1931

Ian King was born in Leeds. A slow left-arm bowler, he played for Warwickshire before joining Essex for the 1957 season. He played 28 matches for the county, taking 34 wickets at an average of 33.70. His best performance was 4 for 25 in the second innings of a victory over Gloucestershire at Romford.

THURSDAY 11th NOVEMBER 1909

Len Parslow was born in Islington. He was a prolific scorer in club cricket and played during the Second World War for a British Empire XI alongside some of the leading cricketers of the day. Parslow played a single first-class match for Essex against Somerset at Taunton in 1946, scoring four and five. He died at Rochford in 1963 at the age of 53.

TUESDAY 12th NOVEMBER 1985

Allan Border finished unbeaten on 152, but could not save Australia from an innings defeat in the first Test against New Zealand in Brisbane. Australia had been bowled out for 179 in the first innings, with Richard Hadlee taking nine wickets, and conceded a massive 374-run deficit. They then fell to 67 for 5 in their second innings before Border found a partner in Greg Matthews and the pair put on 197 together for the sixth wicket. But Matthews fell just before the end of the fourth day, and, although Border continued to resist, the match was over before lunch on day five. Border had batted for seven hours and 42 minutes, facing 301 balls and scoring 20 fours and two sixes.

WEDNESDAY 13th NOVEMBER 1974

John Herringshaw died at Yapton, Sussex, at the age of 82. He was born in Derby and played nine first-class matches for Essex as a slow left-arm bowler in 1921 and 1922, scoring 94 runs at 10.44 and taking nine wickets at an average of 55.33.

MONDAY 14th NOVEMBER 1814

Alfred Adams was born in Saffron Walden. He was one of the earliest stars of Essex cricket, and came to prominence by scoring a massive 279 for Saffron Walden — then the dominant side in the county — against Bishop's Stortford in a club match in July 1837. The innings contained four fives and 25 fours, and was at the time the highest score ever achieved by an individual batsman, beating the 278 scored by W Ward for MCC against Norfolk in 1820. Adams was a formidable player for the Saffron Walden club, and died in the town in 1868.

THURSDAY 15th NOVEMBER 1866

Herbert Burrell was born in Kirtling, Cambridgeshire. He played two first-class matches for Essex in 1895, the county's first season in the championship, scoring 15 runs at 3.75. He had played tennis and cricket for Oxford University and was an ordained minister, later becoming the rector of Balsham in Cambridgeshire and an honorary canon of Ely Cathedral. Burrell died in Cambridge in 1949 aged 82. His younger brother, Reginald John Burrell, also played cricket for Essex.

SUNDAY 16th NOVEMBER 1997

Former Essex wicketkeeper Roy Sheffield died in Auckland, New Zealand, just three days short of his 91st birthday. He was born in Barking and moved to New Zealand in 1938 after a career that saw him play 177 first-class matches for Essex, scoring 3,822 runs at 16.47, with 194 catches and 54 stumpings. He scored one century, against Sussex at Hove in 1936. Off the pitch, Sheffield was an enthusiastic traveller and enjoyed canoeing and other outdoor pursuits. He spent several winters in South America and was once arrested in Paraguay on suspicion of being a Bolivian spy, an incident about which he later wrote a book.

THURSDAY 17th NOVEMBER 1927

Edward Missen died in Colchester at the age of 52. He was born in Cambridge, and played Minor Counties cricket for Cambridgeshire. He has the distinction of being the oldest player to make his debut for Essex, his only appearance coming at the age of 46 against Hampshire at Colchester in 1921. Missen scored eight and 12 as Essex lost by eight wickets.

SUNDAY 18th NOVEMBER 1984

Former Essex captain Harold "Whiz" Morris died in Brighton at the age of 86. He was born in Wanstead and played 240 first-class matches between 1919 and 1932, scoring 6,974 runs at an average of 19.70, with a top score of 166 against Hampshire at Southampton in 1927, when he and Jack Russell put on 233 for the fourth wicket. He was appointed captain after the sacking of Johnny Douglas in 1928 and led the side until his retirement at the end of the 1932 season.

SUNDAY 19th NOVEMBER 1882

Sam Meston was born in Islington. He made his first-class debut with Gloucestershire before appearing in 17 first-class matches for Essex in 1907 and 1908, scoring 476 runs at 17.62. He scored one century for the county, making 130 against Lancashire at Leyton in 1907, including a partnership of 186 for the sixth wicket with Claude Buckenham, as Essex won by an innings. He later moved to Canada and died in Vancouver in 1960. His younger brother, Alexander, also played 12 matches for Essex in the 1920s.

FRIDAY 19th NOVEMBER 1954

Joseph Dixon died in Great Baddow at the age of 59. He was born in Chelmsford and educated at Felsted School. In the First World War he served as a Lieutenant in the Worcestershire Regiment and was awarded the Military Cross in 1917 for his actions at Ovillers in the Somme. Dixon's cricket career had begun before the war and continued until 1922. He played 93 first-class matches for Essex, scoring 2,214 runs at 16.27 and taking 206 wickets at an average of 31.47. He was a capable all-rounder and hit three centuries for the county, with a top score of 173 against Worcestershire in 1922, while he twice took ten wickets in a match. Dixon retired from first-class cricket at the age of 26 to pursue a career in business.

TUESDAY 20th NOVEMBER 1945

Percy Perrin died in Hickling, Norfolk, at the age of 69. He was one on the true greats of Essex cricket, playing for over 30 years, and he remains the only batsman to have scored a triple-century for the county in a championship match. He played in 525 first-class matches for Essex between 1896 and 1928, finally retiring when he was 52 years old, and scored 29,709 runs at 35.92, reaching 1,000 runs in a season on 17 occasions. Perrin made 66 centuries, four times scoring a century in both innings of a match. He was a notoriously slow fielder, which may have cost him the chance of an England cap, although he did take 293 catches in his career. He was appointed an England Test selector in 1926 and was chairman of the selectors from 1930 to 1939.

WEDNESDAY 21st NOVEMBER 1990

Max Osborne was born in Orsett. He made his first-class debut for Essex in 2010 against Bangladesh, taking five wickets in the match, and also played against Durham at the end of the same season. However, he did not play in the first XI in 2011 and was released.

WEDNESDAY 22nd NOVEMBER 1905

Arthur Daer was born in Bishopsgate, London. He was a seam bowler who played 100 first-class matches between 1925 and 1935, taking 195 wickets at an average of 31.70, with a best performance of 6 for 38 against Gloucestershire at Cheltenham in 1933. He also scored 1,469 runs at 14.54. Daer was a publican by trade, and ran the Golden Lion in Romford High Street. He died in Torquay in 1980 at the age of 74. His younger brother, Harry Daer, also played for the county.

THURSDAY 23rd NOVEMBER 1961

Merv Hughes was born in Euroa, in the Australian state of Victoria. He joined the county on an Esso Scholarship in 1983 and played nine matches for the second XI and Under-25 teams that year. He was ineligible to play in the County Championship, but appeared in one first-class match against the touring New Zealanders, taking 2 for 91 and 4 for 71 with the ball and scoring ten and nought. In later years he would become one of the highest-profile players of his generation, playing 53 Tests for Australia and taking 212 Test wickets.

THURSDAY 24th NOVEMBER 1910

Tom Wade was born in Maldon. He played 318 first-class matches for the county between 1929 and 1950, initially as an off-break bowler, taking 48 wickets at 29.54, including a best of 5 for 64 against Somerset in 1929. However, after 1934 he played mainly as a wicketkeeper, taking over from Roy Sheffield as first choice in 1937. Wade was also a useful batsman, scoring 4,972 runs at 14.75, with a top score of 96 against Oxford University in 1932. Aside from his all-round prowess as a cricketer, he was also an accomplished wrestler. He died in Colchester in 1987 at the age of 76.

SATURDAY 25th NOVEMBER 1939

Roger Luckin was born in Pleshey. A left-handed batsman, he played 29 first-class matches in 1962 and 1963, scoring 735 runs at 17.09. He made his highest score of 82 against Middlesex at Brentwood in 1962, when he and Barry Knight put on 206 for the sixth wicket. Luckin later played Minor Counties cricket for Cambridgeshire.

MONDAY 26th NOVEMBER 1877

Philip Morris was born in Kennington. He was a leg-break bowler who played 28 first-class matches for Essex between 1909 and 1924. His appearances were restricted by work commitments, but he achieved considerable success in his limited matches, taking 83 wickets at an average of 22.26 with a best performance of 8 for 106 against Somerset in 1922. Morris took five wickets in an innings on five further occasions, and also scored a half-century, making 55 not out against Surrey in 1922. He died at Hove in 1945 at the age of 67.

THURSDAY 26th NOVEMBER 1970

David Boden was born in Eccleshall, Staffordshire. He played for Middlesex as a youngster before moving to Essex. Boden played three first-class matches for the county in 1992 and 1993, taking only three wickets at an average of 86.00. He later played for Gloucestershire, Staffordshire, and Shropshire.

SUNDAY 26th NOVEMBER 1972

Richard Keigwin died in Polstead, Suffolk, aged 89. He was born in Colchester and played 20 first-class matches for Essex between 1903 and 1919, scoring 455 runs at 15.68 and taking 14 wickets at an average of 45.64. He was a brilliant all-round sportsman who won three hockey caps for England, and represented Cambridge University at hockey, football, and rackets. In the First World War, Keigwin served as a Lieutenant in the Royal Navy Volunteer Reserve and was made a Chevalier de l'Ordre de Leopold (Belgium's highest military award). He later taught modern languages at Clifton College in Bristol and played nine matches for Gloucestershire. He gained acclaim as a translator of Danish literature, especially the fairy tales of Hans Christian Andersen, and became a Knight of the Danish Order of the Dannebrog.

MONDAY 27th NOVEMBER 1933

Bill Dow was born in Glasgow. One of a surprisingly large contingent of Scottish-born players to have found their way into the Essex side, he played two first-class matches for the county in 1958 and 1959, taking four wickets at an average of 42.75. He continued to represent Scotland until 1967, playing at various times in the same side as both Mike Denness and Keith Hardie, the brother of Brian. While playing for Scotland at Dublin in 1965, he took 5 for 9 as Ireland were bowled out for 25.

FRIDAY 27th NOVEMBER 1981

Keith Fletcher captained England in a Test for the first time as they took on India in Bombay (now Mumbai). He had gained a reputation as one of the foremost tacticians in the country, and was appointed to lead England on the winter tour, taking over from Mike Brearley in the wake of a sensational triumph in the previous summer's Ashes series. England lost the first Test heavily, bowled out for 166 and 102, while the remaining five matches produced a succession of high-scoring draws on flat pitches. Fletcher averaged 36 in the series, and presided over a victory against Sri Lanka in a one-off Test at the end of the tour, but he was not reappointed and this winter marked the end of his Test career.

FRIDAY 28th NOVEMBER 1969

Nick Knight was born in Watford. He played 46 first-class matches for Essex between 1991 and 1994, scoring 2,454 runs at an average of 37.18, including seven centuries. His highest score for the county was 157 against Sussex at Chelmsford in 1994. Later that year he left Essex to join Warwickshire, for whom he played for over ten years with great success. Knight also became an England player, appearing in 17 Tests and scoring 719 runs at 23.96 with one century. However, he achieved greater success as an aggressive opening batsman in one-day international cricket. He played exactly 100 one-day internationals and scored 3,637 runs at 40.41, including five centuries. In 1996, playing just his second and third matches, Knight scored centuries on successive days against a Pakistan side that included Waqar Younis and Wasim Akram.

MONDAY 29th NOVEMBER 2010

Alastair Cook reached a superb unbeaten 235 to secure a draw for England in the first Test of the Ashes series against Australia at Brisbane. Cook's innings had actually begun two days earlier, with England trailing by 221 after the first innings. He batted through the whole of the fourth day and well into the fifth, facing 428 balls and hitting 26 fours, as England racked up an incredible 517 for 1 before declaring. His unbroken second-wicket partnership of 329 with Jonathan Trott transformed the character of a series that would go on to be one of triumph both for the England team and for Cook personally.

TUESDAY 30th NOVEMBER 1909

Reg Taylor was born in Southend. He played 206 first-class matches for the county between 1931 and 1946, scoring 6,755 runs at 20.59 and taking 92 wickets with his slow left-arm bowling at an average of 31.88. He scored five centuries, his highest score coming in 1938 when he hit 193 against Sussex at Colchester. During the Second World War, Taylor served as a pilot officer in the RAF. He saw action at the evacuation of Dunkirk and became the first professional cricketer to be awarded the Distinguished Flying Cross. He later moved to South Africa and died in Johannesburg in 1984 at the age of 74.

ESSEX CCC
On This Day

DECEMBER

SUNDAY 1st DECEMBER 1940

Mike Denness was born in Bellshill, Lanarkshire. He joined Essex in 1977 after a 15-year career with Kent, when he had played 28 Tests and became the first Scottish-born player to captain England. He played 83 first-class matches for Essex before his retirement in 1980, scoring 4,050 runs at 31.64, and making six centuries, including a career-best 195 against Leicestershire in 1977. Denness brought much-needed experience and was a regular member of the side that won the county's first championship in 1979. He later served as an ICC match referee.

SUNDAY 2nd DECEMBER 2007

Ravi Bopara played his first Test innings, making just eight before being caught behind off the bowling of Muttiah Muralitharan in the first Test against Sri Lanka at Kandy. Bopara endured a torrid series, making three ducks in five innings as England suffered a 1-0 series defeat. It would be 18 months before he got another chance to play at this level.

MONDAY 3rd DECEMBER 1923

Essex great Trevor Bailey was born in Westcliff-on-Sea. He played 482 first-class matches for the county between 1946 and 1967, scoring 21,460 runs at 34.50 and taking 1,593 wickets at an average of 21.99. His runs included 22 centuries, with a top score of 205 against Sussex at Eastbourne in 1947, while he is one of only two bowlers to have taken all ten wickets in an innings for the county. Bailey took over as county captain in 1961 and led the side for six seasons. He also played 61 Tests for England, scoring 2,290 runs at 29.74 and taking 132 wickets at 29.21. In later years he became a prominent radio broadcaster for the BBC.

MONDAY 3rd DECEMBER 1928

Johnny Douglas was controversially sacked as captain of Essex after 18 years in the post. The side had won only two matches in the previous year and, with Douglas now 46 years old, the club's committee felt that a change of leadership was desirable. Douglas refused to resign, but the committee took matters into its own hands and offered the captaincy to Whiz Morris.

SUNDAY 4th DECEMBER 1988

Five years after turning out for the Essex second XI, Merv Hughes took a Test hat-trick for Australia against the West Indies at Perth. His victims were spread over two days and three overs, with Curtly Ambrose caught behind from the last ball of Hughes's 36th over and Patrick Patterson dismissed from the first ball of his 37th. Patterson was the last wicket of the first innings, and Hughes had to wait for more than a day before the West Indies batted again. He promptly trapped Gordon Greenidge leg-before-wicket with the first ball of the innings to complete a most unusual feat. Hughes went on to take 8 for 87 in the second innings, but he had little support — Geoff Lawson had suffered a fractured jaw when batting against Ambrose — and despite his efforts he would end up on the losing side.

SUNDAY 5th DECEMBER 2010

Alastair Cook was out for 148, his second consecutive century, in the second Test against Australia at Adelaide. His innings had begun late on the first day, and he was finally dismissed on the third day after sharing in century partnerships with Jonathon Trott and Kevin Pietersen. Cook helped England to build a huge lead, and they eventually declared on 620 for 5. They would go on to win the match by an innings and take a 1-0 lead in the Ashes series.

THURSDAY 6th DECEMBER 2001

Essex's James Foster ended on the losing side in his Test debut for England against India at Mohali. He had the satisfaction of not conceding a single bye in 169 overs when India batted, but could manage only nought and five with the bat as England fell to a ten-wicket defeat.

THURSDAY 7th DECEMBER 1967

Adam Seymour was born in Royston, Hertfordshire. He played 14 first-class matches for the county between 1988 and 1991, mainly as an opening batsman, scoring 697 runs at an average of 34.85. His highest score was 157, made against Glamorgan at Cardiff in 1991. Seymour later played for Worcestershire, Cornwall, and Suffolk.

FRIDAY 8th DECEMBER 1905

Rainy Brown was born in Maldon. He played 23 first-class matches for Essex as a slow left-arm bowler between 1924 and 1932, although he was not available for several years because of work commitments with ICI in India. He took 30 wickets at an average of 27.80 and scored 298 runs at 11.92. Brown's best bowling performance was 5 for 55 in the second innings against Somerset at Weston-super-Mare in 1932, although this proved not to be good enough as Somerset's last-wicket pair of Burrough and Luckes put on 45 to snatch victory, with Brown conceding the winning boundary.

TUESDAY 9th DECEMBER 1930

Colin Griffiths was born in Upminster. He played 27 first-class matches for the county between 1951 and 1953, scoring 615 runs at 16.18. He was noted more of the pace of his scoring than the quantity of his runs, and hit the fastest century of the season in 1952. His career was cut short when he went into his family's demolition business.

TUESDAY 9th DECEMBER 1958

Trevor Bailey played one of his most notorious defensive innings, facing 427 balls in seven and a half hours while scoring just 68 for England against Australia in the second innings of the first Test at Brisbane. England had been bowled out for 134 on the first day after winning the toss and batting, so Bailey's rearguard was an attempt to claw his side back into a game in which they were always second favourites. Nevertheless, *Wisden* chastised him for his lack of stroke-play in benign conditions. He was finally ninth out when he played a rare aggressive stroke against Ken Mackay. Australia won the game comfortably and went on to take the series 4-0.

TUESDAY 10th DECEMBER 1918

Harry Daer was born in Hammersmith. He followed his older brother Arthur Daer into the Essex team and played nine first-class matches for the county in 1938 and 1939, taking 11 wickets at an average of 35.18. He ran a sporting goods shop in Romford with another Essex player, Sonny Avery.

SUNDAY 10th DECEMBER 1978

Stephen Peters was born in Harold Wood. He scored a century against Cambridge University on debut as a teenager in 1996, and played 61 more first-class matches before leaving after the 2001 season to join Worcestershire and then Northamptonshire. Peters scored a total of 2,245 first-class runs for Essex at an average of 25.80, hitting one other century — also against Cambridge — in 1997.

SATURDAY 11th DECEMBER 1988

Tim Southee was born in Whangarei, New Zealand. He joined Essex in 2011 to play in the club's Friends Provident Twenty20 campaign alongside international team-mate Scott Styris. Southee took 22 wickets and scored 135 runs in 15 matches, the highlights including a 34-ball innings of 74 against Hampshire, and a match-winning spell of 6 for 16 against Glamorgan.

TUESDAY 12th DECEMBER 1933

Herbert "Bob" Carpenter died at Whipps Cross aged 64. He was born in Cambridge, where his father was a leading player, and first represented Essex in 1888. Carpenter played 262 first-class matches for the county between 1894 and 1920, his last appearance coming at the age of 51. In these games he scored 13,043 runs at 29.50 with 22 centuries and a top score of 199 against Surrey in 1904. Besides being a fine player, Carpenter was also active in coaching and played a key role in the development of many players as Essex established themselves in the first-class game.

FRIDAY 13th DECEMBER 1907

Frederick Fane became the first Essex player to captain England. He had gone on the tour to Australia as vice-captain and took over the captaincy for the first Test at Sydney when Nottinghamshire's Arthur Jones was unable to play through illness. The match ended in a narrow defeat for England by two wickets, as Australia's ninth-wicket pair of Cotter and Hazlitt put on an unbroken partnership of 56. Fane's contribution to the England cause was two and 33. He would also captain the side in the next two matches. England secured a one-wicket victory in the second Test, but lost the series 4-1.

WEDNESDAY 13th DECEMBER 1961

Charles Benham died in Broxburn, West Lothian, aged 81. He was born in Plaistow and played 57 first-class matches for Essex as a fast bowler between 1904 and 1909, taking 65 wickets at 33.47 and scoring 985 runs at 14.25. Benham's best performance came against Sussex in 1908 at Horsham when he took 7 for 60 in a rain-ruined draw. He later played as a club professional in Scotland.

THURSDAY 14th DECEMBER 1978

William Hubble died in Bishop's Waltham, Hampshire, at the age of 80. He was a Leyton-born slow left-arm bowler who played only one first-class match, at Colchester against Cambridge University in 1923. In the first innings he took 0 for 57 and was then bowled by Gubby Allen for a duck. However, he took 2 for 3 to polish off the Cambridge second innings and Essex won the match by seven wickets.

MONDAY 15th DECEMBER 1913

Johnny Douglas scored the only century of his Test career while captaining England against South Africa at Durban. England had bowled out their opponents for 182 on the first day, and Douglas came to the wicket on the second day with his side's reply at 173 for 4. He ended the day unbeaten on 108, having shared half-century partnerships with Phil Mead, Frank Woolley, and Morice Bird and having advanced the total to 419 for 7. He was out on the third day for a hard-grafted 118, made in four and a quarter hours, as England went on to win the match by an innings.

WEDNESDAY 16th DECEMBER 1903

James Richardson was born in Prenton, Cheshire. He played 14 first-class matches for Essex while he was a student at Oxford University between 1924 and 1926. In these he took seven wickets at an average of 36.14 and scored 300 runs at 20.00, with a best score of 82 against Hampshire at Leyton in 1924. Richardson was also an outstanding rugby union player and won five caps for England as a centre in 1928. He died in 1995 at the age of 91.

TUESDAY 16th DECEMBER 1980

Leg-spin bowler Danish Kaneria was born in Karachi, Pakistan. He was already an established Pakistani international when he joined Essex as an overseas player in 2004. Kaneria played 57 first-class matches, taking 307 wickets at an average of 25.09 and scoring 619 runs at 11.46. He took ten wickets in a match on five occasions and also took a hat-trick against Derbyshire in 2009. Kaneria played a major part in the county's one-day successes in 2005, 2006, and 2008. In 2010 he was arrested in connection with an investigation into illegal betting on a cricket match, but he was later released without facing any charges.

SUNDAY 17th DECEMBER 1967

Joe Grant was born in the parish of St James, in Jamaica. As a young pace bowler he had featured in the same Jamaican bowling attack as Courtney Walsh and Patrick Patterson, but was already 33 years old when he joined Essex. He played 15 first-class matches for the county between 2001 and 2003, taking 43 wickets at an average of 31.81, with a best of 5 for 38 against Cambridge University in 2002.

FRIDAY 18th DECEMBER 1925

Stan Eve was born in Stepney. He played club cricket for Upminster and appeared in 32 first-class matches for Essex as an amateur between 1949 and 1957, scoring 1,041 runs at 22.14. Eve's only century came in his second match for the county when he scored 120 against Warwickshire at Leyton, setting up an innings victory.

SATURDAY 19th DECEMBER 1914

Alfred "Sonny" Avery was born in New Beckton. He played 269 first-class matches for Essex between 1935 and 1954, forming a regular opening partnership with Dickie Dodds in the post-war years. He scored 14,137 runs at 33.65, passing 1,000 runs in a season seven times, and hit 25 centuries, including four double centuries — more than any other Essex player apart from Graham Gooch. Avery's highest score was 224, made against Northamptonshire at Northampton in 1952. He was also a talented footballer and played for Leyton in the final of the FA Amateur Cup in 1937.

FRIDAY 19th DECEMBER 1930

Former Essex and England captain Johnny Douglas died in tragic circumstances aged just 48. He had been travelling to Finland with his father on a business trip to purchase timber, when their ship, the *Oberon*, was wrecked off the coast of Denmark. The captain of the ship had been attempting to exchange Christmas greetings with his brother, captain of its sister ship, the *Arcturus*, when the two vessels collided in dense fog and the *Oberon* sank immediately. According to a witness, Douglas might have saved himself, but sought instead to rescue his father. In the event, both men drowned.

SUNDAY 20th DECEMBER 1970

Grant Flower was born in Salisbury (now Harare) in Zimbabwe. He played 39 first-class matches for Essex between 2005 and 2010, appearing alongside his brother Andy in his first two seasons. Grant scored 1,591 runs for the county at 28.41, including four centuries, and took 21 wickets at 35.14. His highest score was 203 against Northamptonshire at Chelmsford in 2007. Grant also played some crucial innings in limited-overs cricket, notably a match-winning 70 not out in the Friends Provident Trophy final in 2008.

FRIDAY 21st DECEMBER 1962

Leonard Graham died in Kensington aged 61. He was born in Leyton and played two first-class matches for Essex in 1926, scoring 14 runs in two completed innings. Graham also played football for Millwall and won two England caps.

WEDNESDAY 22nd DECEMBER 1976

John Lever completed a remarkable Test debut with match figures of 10 for 70 as England defeated India by an innings and 25 runs in the first Test in Delhi. Lever polished off the Indian tail in the second innings, taking 3 for 24 to follow his 7 for 46 in the first innings. He had also made an improbable 53 when England batted. It was later suggested that Lever had applied Vaseline to the ball to gain an unfair advantage, but his team-mates maintained that Lever's success in the first innings had come with a "rogue" substitute ball which swung prodigiously of its own accord.

SUNDAY 23rd DECEMBER 1906

Lewis Lywood was born in Walthamstow. He played for Surrey in 1927 and 1928 before making his Essex debut in 1930. He played in Essex's home matches against Worcestershire and Northamptonshire that year, taking two wickets at an average of 41.50. Lywood died in Caterham, Surrey, in 1971 at the age of 64.

SATURDAY 24th DECEMBER 1898

Hubert Waugh was born in West Ham. He played eight first-class matches for Essex as an amateur between 1919 and 1929, scoring 251 runs at 15.68 and taking four wickets at 42.00. Waugh scored one century, against Glamorgan at Leyton in 1928. He later played Minor Counties cricket for Suffolk, and played in the Minor Counties side against the touring New Zealanders in 1937. He died in 1954 in Dollis Hill, Middlesex.

FRIDAY 25th DECEMBER 1868

George Higgins was born in Mile End. He played nine first-class matches for the county in 1894 and 1895, scoring 306 runs at an average of 18.00. Higgins played in Essex's first ever match in the County Championship, against Warwickshire at Edgbaston in 1895, and had the distinction of becoming the county's first centurion in the championship, scoring 118 in the first innings of that match.

TUESDAY 25th DECEMBER 1984

Alastair Cook was born in Gloucester. He made his debut for Essex in 2003 and became a first-team regular in the following season. In 2005 he scored 1,466 runs and announced himself as a high-class player with an innings of 214 against the touring Australians. By the end of the 2011 season, Cook had played 64 first-class matches for the county, scoring 4,784 runs at an average of 44.71, including 12 centuries. He was awarded an England central contract after the 2006 season, after which his appearances for Essex became outnumbered by his appearances for the national side. Cook captained England in Bangladesh in early 2010 and became a national hero after scoring three centuries and averaging 127.66 in the Ashes series the following winter. In 2011 he was appointed England captain for one-day internationals.

MONDAY 26th DECEMBER 1887

Percy Campbell was born in West Ham. He played 13 first-class matches for Essex between 1911 and 1919, batting in the lower middle-order and scoring 270 runs at an average of 14.21. He died in South Woodford in 1960 at the age of 72.

TUESDAY 27th DECEMBER 1932

Graham Horrex was born in Goodmayes. He played seven first-class matches for Essex in 1956 and 1957, scoring 141 runs at 10.84. His top score of 41 was made against Australia at Southend in 1956, when he opened the batting against Ray Lindwall and Keith Miller. Horrex later played for Preston in the Northern Cricket League and became an international squash referee.

WEDNESDAY 28th DECEMBER 1898

Jim Cutmore was born in Walthamstow. An opening batsman, he played 342 first-class matches for the county between 1924 and 1936, scoring 15,937 runs at 28.61 and passing 1,000 runs for the season in 11 consecutive years between 1925 and 1935. He hit 15 centuries, with a highest score of 238 not out in a drawn match against Gloucestershire at Bristol in 1927. Some of Cutmore's most valuable performances came in tight finishes: he guided Essex home by two wickets against Kent in 1934, scoring an unbeaten 97 out of 166 for 8, while his 36 not out against Leicestershire in the same season secured victory by the same margin. Cutmore also had a fine voice and worked for a while in music hall. He died in Brentwood in 1985 aged 86.

TUESDAY 28th DECEMBER 2010

Alastair Cook scored 118 as England built a lead in the second Test against South Africa in Durban. Cook resumed his innings on 31 and shared in a partnership of 142 for the fourth wicket with Paul Collingwood. He was dismissed in the final session after batting for over six and a half hours and hitting 11 fours. On the following day Ian Bell completed a century of his own and England declared on 574 for 9, 231 runs ahead. South Africa were then dismissed for 133 and England won by an innings.

SATURDAY 29th DECEMBER 1891

Alf Taylor was born in West Ham. He played two first-class matches for Essex in 1923, taking a single wicket at a cost of 77 runs. Taylor's last match was against Surrey at Leyton, and he made a pair as Essex lost by an innings.

THURSDAY 30th DECEMBER 1948

Steve Dinsdale was born in Buckhurst Hill. He was a left-handed batsman who played five first-class matches for the county in 1970, scoring 97 runs at 13.85 with a highest score of 29 against Hampshire at Bournemouth. Dinsdale also played first-class cricket for Rhodesia and Transvaal.

TUESDAY 31st DECEMBER 1935

John Wright was born in Colchester. He played two first-class matches for the county in 1962 and a further two in 1967 — all at his home ground at Colchester, where he was captain of the Colchester and East Essex club. Wright scored 60 runs at an average of ten, with a highest score of 40 on his debut against Northamptonshire.